SKINNY PASTA

SKINNY COOKING

Skinny Pasta

SUE SPITLER

SURREY BOOKS

CHICAGO

SKINNY PASTA is published by Surrey Books, Inc.
230 E. Ohio St., Suite 120, Chicago, IL 60611.

Second edition: 1 2 3 4 5

This book is manufactured in the United States of America.

Library of Congress Cataloging-in-Publication data:

Spitler, Sue.
    Skinny pasta / Sue Spitler.—2nd ed.
    176p. cm.
    Includes index.
    ISBN 1-57284-008-0 (paper)
    1. Cookery (Pasta) 2. Low-cholesterol diet—Recipes 3. Low-fat diet—
Recipes. 4. Low-calorie diet—Recipes. I. Title.
TX809.M17S65 1996
641.8'22—dc20   96-326250
                                                  CIP

Editorial and production: *Bookcrafters, Inc., Chicago*
Art Director: *Joan Sommers Design, Chicago*
Cover and interior illustrations by *Mona Daly*

For free catalog and prices on quantity purchases, contact Surrey Books at the
address above.

This title is distributed to the trade by Publishers Group West.

Titles in the "Skinny" Cookbooks Series:

Skinny Beef   *Skinny Pasta*
Skinny Chicken   *Skinny Pizzas*
Skinny Chocolate   *Skinny Potatoes*
Skinny Comfort Foods   *Skinny Sandwiches*
Skinny Cookies, Cakes, & Sweets *Skinny Sauces & Marinades*
Skinny Grilling   *Skinny Seafood*
Skinny Italian Cooking   *Skinny Soups*
Skinny Mexican Cooking   *Skinny Spices*
Skinny One-Pot Meals   *Skinny Vegetarian Entrées*

To Aunt Fay

remembering blueberry picking and other
special times we've shared!

Acknowledgments

Thank you, Susan Schwartz, for agreeing that *Skinny Pasta* was a perfect addition to the "Skinny Cookbooks" series. To chef-associate Cheryl Flynn, applause for having chopped, stirred, sauteed, and simmered her way through another cookbook in my test kitchen! Cheers to my capacious friend, Peg Sullivan, who consumed miles of pasta in total support of this project. Great appreciation is extended to Linda R. Yoakam for her helpfulness and expertise in providing nutritional information and computations. And, a sincere thank-you to editor Gene DeRoin, who worked expertly behind the scenes to produce a worthy cookbook.

CONTENTS

INTRODUCTION

Few food trends have been as popular or enduring as pasta. Pasta is IN—pasta is *definitely* here to stay.

A staple in many of the world's cuisines, pasta has many claims to culinary fame. It tastes fabulous. Pasta is fun, with numerous shapes and varieties to choose among. Boasting versatility, pasta can be served as an appetizer, soup, entree, casserole, salad, luncheon dish, or even a quick stir-fry.

Pasta is fast and simple to prepare.

Most importantly, pasta is *healthy:* a 2-ounce portion of pasta packs a nutritious 4 to 8 grams of protein, 42 grams of carbohydrate, 80 milligrams of potassium, 10 to 15 percent of the U.S. RDA of riboflavin, niacin, and iron, and 35 percent RDA of thiamine. Impressively, 2 ounces of pasta contain only 210 calories and, if egg free, 0 to 1 gram of fat and 0 milligrams of cholesterol. Unfortunately, these nutritional attributes are often corrupted by what is added to the pasta—calorie- and fat-laden sauces with sausage and red meats, generous amounts of olive oil, cheeses, and cream.

In *Skinny Pasta* the nutritional bonuses of pasta are enhanced in recipes that include healthful low-calorie, low-fat ingredients. In adherence to guidelines established by the American Heart Association, the following nutritional criteria were followed in creating the recipes for *Skinny Pasta:*

TYPE OF RECIPE	MAXIMUM AMOUNTS PER SERVING		
	Calories	Cholesterol (mg)	Sodium (mg)
First-Course Pasta, Soups	200	50	600
Main-Dish Soups, Entrees, Salads (with meat)	600	150	800
Main-Dish Soups, Entrees, Salads (meatless)	500	125	800
Side-Dish Pasta, Salads	200	50	600
Sauces	200	50	800

All recipes are low in fat, not exceeding the 30 percent of calories-from-fat guidelines recommended by the American Heart Association. The sauce recipes may individually exceed 30 percent of calories from fat but are 30 percent or less when combined with a 2-ounce serving of pasta.

Each recipe includes a nutritional analysis, detailing calories and fat, saturated fat, cholesterol, carbohydrate, protein, and sodium amounts. Percent of calories from fat is included as well as diabetic exchanges. Please understand that the nutritional data are not infallible. Although they should prove very useful in planning meals, especially for those on diet programs, bear in mind that they were developed according to the following guidelines:

1. Recipes were analyzed, for the most part, using purchased dry pasta, which generally contains no eggs, as opposed to homemade pasta.

2. Where alternative ingredients or amounts are listed, the first ingredient or amount was used in our calculations.

3. Optional, "to taste," and garnish ingredients were not figured into the nutritional data.

4. Although every effort was made to provide accurate data, sizes of vegetables, specific components of packaged ingredients, differences among brands, and other variables make it impossible to assure total accuracy.

To achieve optimal nutrition and low fat percentages, we emphasized fresh versus processed ingredients and used the many excellent reduced-sodium, no-salt-added, reduced-fat, low-fat, and fat-free ingredients currently available. The use of olive and vegetable oil cooking sprays for sauteing greatly reduces or eliminates the amounts of oil or fat needed in recipes. You'll find that flavors are fresh, with an integrity unhampered by additives and artificial flavorings. Fresh and dried herbs further enhance natural flavors and create new taste combinations.

Variety abounds in this collection of 110 pasta recipes. As might be anticipated, many of the recipes are Italian in origin, taking a "skinny" approach to traditional favorites such as Chicken with Fettuccine Alfredo, Chicken Cacciatore, Linguine with White Clam Sauce, Sausage Lasagne, and Italian Meatball Soup. More adventurous preparations include Chicken and Sweet Potato Ravioli with Curry Sauce, Fettuccine with Pork, Greens, and Caramelized Onions, Grilled Summer Vegetables in Pasta Nests, and Salmon with Cilantro Pesto Fettuccine.

Borrowing ideas from other cultures and cuisines results in flavorful renditions of Beef Bourguignonne with Pasta, Chicken and Pasta Marengo, Chicken Fricassee with Pappardelle, Pasta Santa Fe, Jerk Chicken and Shrimp with Linguine, Mexican-Style Lasagne, and many more. As Asian noodle dishes are very popular and ingredients have become available, a brief section of these recipes has been included. And although not technically a pasta, this cookbook did not seem complete without a risotto chapter.

Pasta shapes and varieties are numerous in supermarkets. If you have access to an Italian market, the choice becomes even more abundant. Although light or fine-textured sauces are most often served with flat pastas and heartier, chunky sauces are served with tube or shaped pastas, the real rule is to serve the pasta you like! Feel free to substitute *any* desired pasta in recipes—experiment, enjoy!

PASTA GLOSSARY

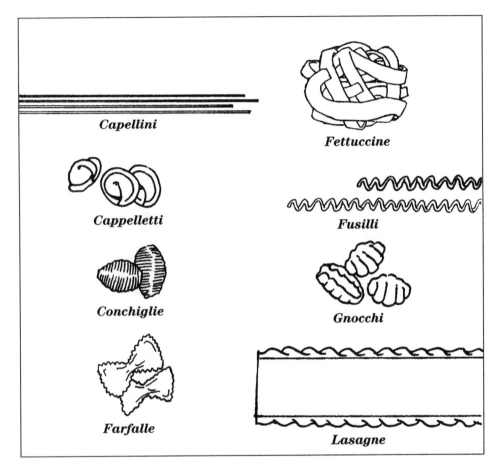

Capellini

Fettuccine

Cappelletti

Fusilli

Conchiglie

Gnocchi

Farfalle

Lasagne

•**Capellini** Very fine, round strands of pasta often called "angel's hair."

•**Cappelletti** Like tortelloni, but made from small squares rather than rounds of pasta. The name means "little hats," which the pasta resembles.

•**Conchiglie** "Conch shells."

•**Farfalle** Pasta shaped like "bow ties," or "butterflies."

•**Fettuccine** The classic flat pasta, also called "ribbons."

•**Fusilli** Pasta with a "spiral," or "spring," shape; can be in long or short pieces.

•**Gnocchi** Similar to conchiglie, but the shells have rippled edges.

•**Lasagne** The widest of the flat noodles, with straight or rippled edges. Most often layered in lasagne or casseroles.

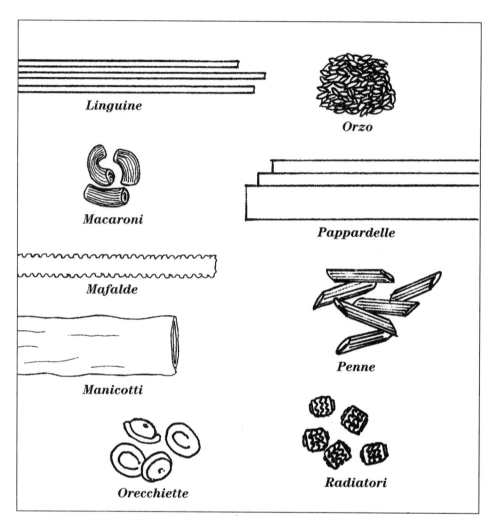

•**Linguine**   Long, flat strands of pasta, "little tongues," that are narrower than fettuccine.

•**Macaroni**   Short, curved pasta tubes.

•**Mafalde**   Flat pasta of moderate width, with rippled edges.

•**Manicotti**   Large pasta tubes for stuffing; tubes can be smooth or ridged.

•**Orecchiette**   Rounded, disk-shaped pasta also called "little ears."

•**Orzo**   A small rice- or oat-shaped pasta most commonly used in soups, salads, and casseroles.

•**Pappardelle**   A flat pasta that measures about 1 inch in width.

•**Penne, or Mostaccioli**   Smooth or ridged pasta tubes, similar to ziti, with angled ends that resemble pen "nibs"; also called "quills" and "pens."

•**Radiatori**   This pasta resembles the radiators for which they are named. Also called "nuggets."

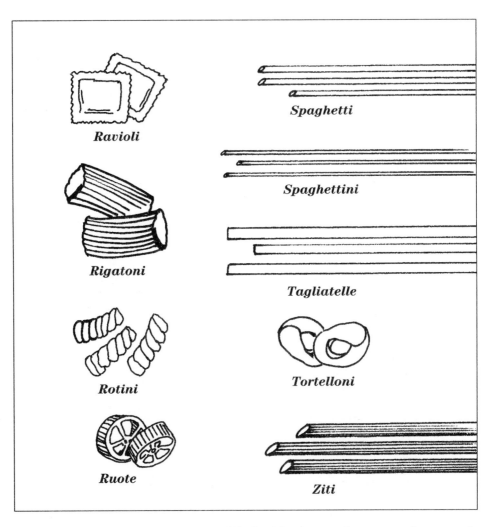

•**Ravioli** Small squares of pasta filled with seasoned meat or cheese and sealed. Ravioli can be made by hand or in special molds.

•**Rigatoni** Ridged tubes, similar in size to ziti.

•**Rotini** Similar to fusilli, with a "corkscrew" shape.

•**Ruote, or Rotelle** Pasta shaped like round "wheels."

•**Spaghetti** The classic long, round strands of pasta.

•**Spaghettini** A thin spaghetti.

•**Tagliatelle** A thin, flat pasta similar to fettuccine.

•**Tortelloni** Also known as "little twists" and "little dumplings." Small rounds of pasta are filled with seasoned meat or cheese, sealed, and folded.

•**Ziti** Pasta tubes. The tubes can be smooth or ridged, long or short.

HOMEMADE PASTA

Fresh pasta dough is not difficult to make. A pasta machine is a very simple and expedient way of kneading, rolling, and cutting the dough, producing a high-quality pasta. Rolling and cutting the dough by hand is somewhat more difficult, requiring practice to make thin, delicate pasta. Follow cooking directions in Step 6 carefully. Fresh pasta cooks very quickly—much more quickly than purchased fresh or dried pasta.

4 Entree Servings

1½ cups all-purpose flour
2 large eggs

1. Mound flour on cutting board, making a well in center. Drop eggs into center of well.

2. Break egg yolks and mix eggs with fork. While mixing eggs, gradually start to incorporate flour into the eggs. As flour is incorporated, it will be necessary to move the mound of flour toward the center, using your hands. Continue mixing until all or almost all flour has been incorporated, forming a soft, but not sticky, ball of dough.

Machine Kneading and Cutting

3. *To knead dough using a pasta machine,* set machine rollers on widest setting. Cut dough into 2 equal pieces. Lightly flour outside of 1 piece, and pass it through machine. Fold piece of dough into thirds; pass it through machine again, inserting open edges (not the fold) of dough first. Repeat folding and rolling 8 to 12 times or until dough feels smooth and satiny; *lightly flour dough only if it begins to feel sticky.*

   Move machine rollers to next narrower setting. Pass dough (do not fold dough any longer) through rollers, beginning to roll out and stretch dough. Move machine rollers to next narrower setting; pass dough through rollers. Continue process until pasta is as thin as wished. (Often the narrowest setting on machine makes pasta too thin; 1 or 2 settings from the end is usually best.) *Lightly flour dough if it begins to feel even slightly sticky at any time.*

   To cut dough using a pasta machine, set cutting rollers for width of pasta desired; pass dough through cutters. Arrange cut pasta in single layer on lightly floured surface.

   Repeat above procedures with second piece of dough.

Hand Kneading and Cutting

4. *To knead dough by hand,* knead on lightly floured surface until dough is smooth and satiny, about 10 minutes. Cover dough lightly with damp towel and let rest 10 minutes.

   Place dough on lightly floured surface. Starting in center of dough, roll with rolling pin from center to edge. Continue rolling, always from center to edge (to keep dough as round as possible) until dough is about 1/16 inch thick. *Lightly flour dough if it begins to feel even slightly sticky at any time.*

   To cut dough by hand, flour top of dough lightly and roll up. Cut into desired widths with sharp knife. Immediately unroll cut pasta to keep noodles from sticking together, and arrange in single layer on lightly floured surface.

5. Pasta can be cooked fresh, or it can be frozen or dried to be cooked later. To freeze pasta, place in heavy plastic freezer bag and freeze. To dry pasta, let stand on floured surface (or hang over rack) until completely dried. (Be sure pasta is completely dried or it will turn moldy in storage.) Store at room temperature in airtight container.

6. To cook fresh, frozen, or dried pasta, heat 4 to 5 quarts lightly salted (optional) water to boiling. Add pasta and begin testing for doneness as soon as water returns to boil. Cooking time will vary from 0 to 2 minutes once water has returned to boil.

Nutritional Data

PER SERVING		EXCHANGES	
Calories	208	Milk	0.0
% Calories from fat	13	Veg.	0.0
Fat (gm)	3	Fruit	0.0
Sat. fat (gm)	0.8	Bread	2.5
Cholesterol (mg)	106.5	Meat	0.0
Sodium (mg)	32	Fat	0.5
Protein (gm)	8		
Carbohydrate (gm)	36.1		

Note: Fresh, homemade pasta can be used with any recipe, but it will result in a higher cholesterol count than stated with the recipe, in some cases exceeding the guidelines shown on page xii. A few of the recipes that will exceed the guidelines if fresh pasta is used include: Beef Bourguignonne with Pasta, Jerk Chicken and Shrimp with Linguine, Fettuccine with Pork, Greens, and Caramelized Onions, Pasta Pizza, Shrimp and Artichoke Ravioli, and Tagliatelle with Chicken Liver Sauce.

1
FIRST COURSE

M any of the first course recipes can appropriately be served as light luncheon entrees, or doubled in amount for a dinner entree. The Ricotta-Stuffed Shells with Spinach Pesto and Mushrooms Stuffed with Orzo can be served as delightful hors d'oeuvre offerings. See the Soups and Salads chapters for other first-course recipes.

MUSHROOMS STUFFED WITH ORZO

Enjoy flavor accents of tangy goat's cheese and a trio of fresh herbs.

4 Servings (3 mushrooms each)

12 large mushrooms
   Vegetable cooking spray
 1 tablespoon finely chopped medium shallots
 2 cloves garlic, minced
 1 tablespoon finely chopped fresh basil leaves,
   or 1 teaspoon dried
 2 teaspoons finely chopped fresh oregano
   leaves, *or* 1/2 teaspoon dried
1/2 teaspoon finely chopped fresh thyme leaves,
   or 1/8 teaspoon dried
1/4 cup (2 ounces) orzo, cooked
 1 tablespoon goat's cheese, *or* reduced-fat
   cream cheese
   Basil, *or* oregano sprigs

1. Remove stems from mushrooms and chop coarsely. Reserve caps. Spray medium skillet with cooking spray; heat over medium heat until hot. Saute mushroom stems 2 to 3 minutes. Add shallots, garlic, and chopped herbs; saute until shallot is almost tender, about 3 minutes. Stir in orzo and goat's cheese; cook until orzo is warm, 1 to 2 minutes.

2. Heat oven to 350° F. Spoon orzo filling into mushroom caps and place in 13 x 9-inch baking pan. Bake, covered with aluminum foil, until mushroom caps are tender, about 15 minutes. Remove foil and bake 5 minutes longer.

3. Arrange mushrooms on serving plates; garnish with herb sprigs. Serve warm.

Nutritional Data

PER SERVING		EXCHANGES	
Calories	86	Milk	0.0
% Calories from fat	24	Veg.	1.0
Fat (gm)	2.6	Fruit	0.0
Sat. fat (gm)	0.6	Bread	0.5
Cholesterol (mg)	3.4	Meat	0.0
Sodium (mg)	18	Fat	0.5
Protein (gm)	5.3		
Carbohydrate (gm)	13		

CRANBERRY CHEESE WONTONS

Dried cranberries and ginger root add a lively accent to these unusual cheese wontons. When fried at the correct temperature, deep-fried foods absorb almost no fat.

6 Servings (4 each)

- ³/₄ package (8-ounce size) fat-free cream cheese
- 3 tablespoons chopped dried cranberries
- 2 tablespoons finely chopped chives
- ¹/₂ to ³/₄ teaspoon minced ginger root
- 1 tablespoon minced parsley
  Salt and white pepper, to taste
- 24 wonton wrappers
- 1 egg white, beaten
  Vegetable oil, for frying
- ¹/₃ cup jalapeño jelly, heated

1. Mix cream cheese, cranberries, chives, ginger root, and parsley in small bowl; season to taste with salt and white pepper.

2. Spoon ¹/₂ tablespoon filling on wonton wrapper; brush edges of wrapper with egg white. Fold wrapper in half and press edges to seal. Repeat with remaining filling, wrappers, and egg white.

3. Heat 2 inches of oil in large saucepan to 375° F. Fry wontons, 6 to 8 at a time, until golden, 1 to 2 minutes. Drain very well on paper toweling. Serve hot with jalapeño jelly or tamari soy sauce.

Nutritional Data

PER SERVING		EXCHANGES	
Calories	182	Milk	0.0
% Calories from fat	10	Veg.	0.0
Fat (gm)	1.9	Fruit	1.0
Sat. fat (gm)	0.3	Bread	1.0
Cholesterol (mg)	4	Meat	1.0
Sodium (mg)	368	Fat	0.0
Protein (gm)	7.9		
Carbohydrate (gm)	31.6		

"LITTLE EARS" WITH GARLIC AND ARTICHOKES

The flavors of the garlic and artichokes become sweet and mellow when roasted. The garlic becomes the sauce for this appetizing first course. Because of its shape, orecchiette are often called "little ears." Other pasta shapes can be substituted.

4 Servings

1 can (15½ ounces) artichoke hearts, drained, rinsed
  Olive oil cooking spray
2 bulbs garlic
2 teaspoons olive oil
1 cup (4 ounces) orecchiette ("little ears"), cooked, warm
2 teaspoons grated Romano cheese
1 tablespoon finely chopped parsley
⅛ teaspoon salt (optional)
¼ teaspoon pepper
  Radicchio
1 ounce feta cheese, crumbled

1. Heat oven to 400° F. Cut artichoke hearts into halves and place, cut sides down, in small baking pan; spray with cooking spray. Cut a scant ½ inch off tops of garlic bulbs, exposing ends of cloves. Wrap garlic bulbs loosely in aluminum foil and place in same pan. Bake artichoke hearts, uncovered, and garlic until garlic is very soft, about 15 minutes.

2. Cool garlic slightly; squeeze pulp into small bowl and mix with olive oil. Combine garlic mixture and pasta; mix in artichoke hearts and remaining ingredients, except radicchio and feta cheese, and toss.

3. Arrange radicchio leaves on small serving plates; spoon pasta over. Sprinkle with feta cheese.

Nutritional Data

PER SERVING		EXCHANGES	
Calories	203	Milk	0.0
% Calories from fat	23	Veg.	2.0
Fat (gm)	5.3	Fruit	0.0
Sat. Fat (gm)	1.9	Bread	1.5
Cholesterol (mg)	8.7	Meat	0.0
Sodium (mg)	263	Fat	1.0
Protein (gm)	9.5		
Carbohydrate (gm)	31.8		

CHICKEN TORTELLONI WITH TOMATO-MUSHROOM SAUCE

Dry sherry and thyme accent the richly textured Tomato-Mushroom Sauce.

6 Servings

Vegetable cooking spray
1/4 cup chopped onions
1 small leek (white part only), very thinly sliced
3 tablespoons chopped shallots
4 large mushrooms, chopped
1/4 cup dry sherry, *or* low-salt chicken broth
1/4 teaspoon salt
1/4 teaspoon pepper
1 cup low-salt chicken broth
1 medium tomato, chopped
1 1/2 to 2 teaspoons dried thyme leaves
2 bay leaves
1 package (9 ounces) chicken tortelloni, cooked, warm
2 tablespoons drained capers (optional)

1. Spray medium saucepan with cooking spray; heat over medium heat until hot. Saute onions, leek, shallots, and mushrooms until very soft, 7 to 10 minutes. Add sherry; cook over high heat until liquid is almost absorbed, 2 to 3 minutes. Stir in salt and pepper.

2. Add chicken broth, tomato, thyme and bay leaves to saucepan; heat to boiling. Reduce heat and simmer, uncovered, until tomato is very soft, about 15 minutes; discard bay leaves. Process mixture in food proces-

sor or blender until smooth. Return to saucepan; cook over medium heat until hot.

3. Spoon sauce over tortelloni; sprinkle with capers.

Nutritional Data

PER SERVING		EXCHANGES	
Calories	167	Milk	0.0
% Calories from fat	16	Veg.	1.0
Fat (gm)	3.1	Fruit	0.0
Sat. Fat (gm)	1.5	Bread	1.5
Cholesterol (mg)	20.2	Meat	0.0
Sodium (mg)	219	Fat	0.5
Protein (gm)	8.7		
Carbohydrate (gm)	25.8		

RICOTTA-STUFFED SHELLS WITH SPINACH PESTO

Pesto sauces are traditionally served at room temperature. Spinach Pesto can be made up to 1 week in advance and refrigerated. Before serving, let it stand until room temperature, or microwave in glass bowl at medium setting until softened, about 30 seconds.

4 Servings (3 shells each)

Vegetable cooking spray
1/4 cup finely chopped onions
2 to 3 cloves garlic, minced
1/2 teaspoon dried basil leaves
1/2 cup chopped fresh spinach
3/4 cup low-fat ricotta cheese
1/4 teaspoon ground nutmeg
1/4 teaspoon salt
1/4 teaspoon pepper
12 conchiglie (jumbo pasta shells), about 4 ounces, cooked
Spinach Pesto (recipe follows)
2 tablespoons chopped red or green bell peppers, roasted or raw
Basil sprigs

1. Spray medium skillet with cooking spray; saute onions, garlic, and dried basil until onions are tender, 3 to 4 minutes. Add spinach; cook over medium heat until spinach is wilted, about 5 minutes.

2. Heat oven to 350° F. Mix spinach mixture into cheese; stir in nutmeg, salt, and pepper. Stuff mixture into shells; place in baking pan. Bake, covered, until hot through, about 20 minutes.

3. Arrange shells on small serving plates; spoon Spinach Pesto over shells or serve on the side. Sprinkle with bell peppers; garnish with basil sprigs.

Spinach Pesto

Makes 4 servings (about 2 tablespoons each)

    1 cup fresh spinach, loosely packed
    3 tablespoons finely chopped fresh basil leaves,
        or 1 tablespoon dried
1 to 2 cloves garlic, minced
    1 tablespoon grated Parmesan cheese
    2 teaspoons olive oil
1 to 2 teaspoons lemon juice

1. Process all ingredients, except lemon juice, in food processor or blender until smooth. Season with lemon juice.

2. Let stand 2 to 3 hours for flavors to blend, or refrigerate until serving time. Serve at room temperature.

Nutritional Data

PER SERVING		EXCHANGES	
Calories	178	Milk	0.0
% Calories from fat	24	Veg.	1.0
Fat (gm)	4.7	Fruit	0.0
Sat. Fat (gm)	0.8	Bread	1.5
Cholesterol (mg)	7.2	Meat	0.5
Sodium (mg)	216	Fat	0.5
Protein (gm)	9.5		
Carbohydrate (gm)	24.6		

GRILLED SUMMER VEGETABLES IN PASTA NESTS

*For attractive serving, the linguine is shaped into small
nests to contain the medley of roasted vegetables.*

8 Servings

    3 tablespoons olive oil, divided
    2 tablespoons balsamic vinegar, *or* red wine
       vinegar
    1 teaspoon lemon juice
    3 cloves garlic, minced, divided
    2 teaspoons crushed caraway seed
 $1/4$ teaspoon salt
 $1/4$ teaspoon pepper
    1 medium eggplant, peeled, cut into
       1-inch pieces
    1 medium zucchini, sliced
    1 medium red or green bell pepper, cut into
       1-inch pieces
    1 small red onion, cut into 1-inch wedges
       Vegetable cooking spray
   12 ounces linguine, cooked, warm
    1 tablespoon minced parsley

1. Mix 2 tablespoons of oil, vinegar, lemon juice, 2 cloves of garlic, caraway seed, salt, and pepper; pour over combined vegetables in shallow
glass baking dish. Let stand, covered, 30 to 60 minutes.

2. Heat oven to 400° F. Spray 2 jelly roll pans with cooking spray; arrange
vegetables in single layer on pans. Bake until vegetables are browned
and just tender, about 20 minutes.

3. Toss linguine with remaining 1 tablespoon oil, parsley, and remaining 1
clove garlic. Shape linguine into 8 small "nests"; spoon vegetables into
"nests."

Nutritional Data

PER SERVING		EXCHANGES	
Calories	197	Milk	0.0
% Calories from fat	30	Veg.	1.5
Fat (gm)	6.8	Fruit	0.0
Sat. Fat (gm)	0.8	Bread	1.5
Cholesterol (mg)	0	Meat	0.0
Sodium (mg)	138	Fat	1.0
Protein (gm)	6.4		
Carbohydrate (gm)	29.1		

MIXED VEGETABLE FETTUCCINE

Roasting is an effortless way to cook many vegetables at the same time, also enhancing their natural flavors.

6 Servings

2 sweet potatoes, cut into scant 1/2-inch slices
1 yellow summer squash, sliced
1 large tomato, cut into 8 wedges
1 green bell pepper, cut into 3/4-inch slices
4 green onions, very thinly sliced
   Olive oil cooking spray
1/4 cup cider vinegar
2 tablespoons olive oil, *or* vegetable oil
1 teaspoon lemon juice
1 tablespoon finely chopped parsley
1 tablespoon finely chopped fresh oregano
   leaves, *or* 1 teaspoon dried
1 tablespoon finely chopped fresh tarragon
   leaves, *or* 1 teaspoon dried
8 ounces fettuccine, cooked, room temperature
1 tablespoon grated Parmesan cheese

1. Heat oven to 400° F. Arrange vegetables on jelly roll pan; spray generously with cooking spray and toss. Bake until vegetables are browned and just tender, 20 to 25 minutes.

2. Mix vinegar, olive oil, lemon juice, and herbs; drizzle over warm roasted vegetables and toss. Spoon over pasta and toss; sprinkle with Parmesan cheese.

Nutritional Data

PER SERVING		EXCHANGES	
Calories	200	Milk	0.0
% Calories from fat	26	Veg.	1.0
Fat (gm)	6.4	Fruit	0.0
Sat. Fat (gm)	0.8	Bread	2.0
Cholesterol (mg)	0.8	Meat	0.0
Sodium (mg)	89	Fat	1.0
Protein (gm)	6.8		
Carbohydrate (gm)	34.8		

PASTA PIZZA

◆

Pizza flavors on a pasta crust!

6 Servings

   4 sun-dried tomatoes
      Hot water
   4 ounces reduced-fat turkey Italian sausage
   1 cup sliced mushrooms
 1/2 cup chopped onions
   1 tablespoon finely chopped fresh oregano
      leaves, *or* 1 teaspoon dried
   1 tablespoon finely chopped fresh basil leaves,
      or 1 teaspoon dried
 1/4 teaspoon salt (optional)
 1/4 teaspoon pepper
      Vegetable cooking spray
   6 ounces fettuccine, cooked
   1 egg white, beaten
   1 tablespoon finely chopped parsley
1 1/2 ounces goat's cheese, *or* reduced-fat
      cream cheese

1. Place tomatoes in small bowl; pour hot water over to cover. Let stand until tomatoes are softened, about 15 minutes; drain. Chop tomatoes.

2. Cook turkey in medium skillet over medium heat until browned; drain and crumble. Drain any excess fat from skillet. Add mushrooms, onions, and tomatoes and saute until tender, about 5 minutes. Stir in oregano, basil, salt, and pepper.

3. Spray 10-inch skillet with cooking spray; heat over medium heat until hot. Combine fettuccine, egg white, and parsley; place in skillet and pat into an even layer with pancake turner.

4. Spoon turkey-vegetable mixture in even layer over pasta; dot with cheese. Cook over medium to medium-high heat, covered, 5 minutes. Uncover and cook 5 minutes more or until pasta is lightly browned on bottom. Cut into wedges to serve.

Nutritional Data

PER SERVING		EXCHANGES	
Calories	168	Milk	0.0
% Calories from fat	29	Veg.	2.0
Fat (gm)	5.7	Fruit	0.0
Sat. Fat (gm)	1.6	Bread	1.0
Cholesterol (mg)	21.6	Meat	0.5
Sodium (mg)	281	Fat	0.5
Protein (gm)	9.1		
Carbohydrate (gm)	21.6		

MUSHROOM RAVIOLI WITH RED PEPPER SALSA

Ravioli are very easy to make using purchased wonton wrappers (found in the produce or refrigerated sections of supermarkets). Colorful Red Pepper Salsa is a perfect complement to the mushroom-filled pasta.

4 Servings (3 ravioli each)

  Vegetable cooking spray
1 cup sliced mushrooms
2 tablespoons chopped shallots, *or* green onions
1 clove garlic, minced
1 tablespoon finely chopped parsley
$1/8$ teaspoon salt
$1/8$ teaspoon pepper
24 wonton wrappers
  Water
  Red Pepper Salsa (recipe follows)

1. Spray large skillet with cooking spray; heat over medium heat until hot. Saute mushrooms, shallots, and garlic until tender, about 7 minutes; stir in parsley, salt, and pepper. Transfer mixture to food processor or blender; process until finely chopped but not smooth.

2. Spoon about 2 teaspoons mushroom mixture in center of 1 wonton wrapper; brush edges of wrapper with water. Top with a second wonton wrapper, and press edges together to seal. Repeat with remaining wonton wrappers and mushroom mixture.

3. Heat about 2 quarts water to boiling in large saucepan; add 4 to 6 wonton ravioli. Reduce heat and simmer, uncovered, until ravioli float to surface and are *al dente,* 3 to 4 minutes. Remove ravioli with slotted spoon; repeat cooking procedure with remaining ravioli. Serve with Red Pepper Salsa.

Red Pepper Salsa

Makes 4 servings (about 1/4 cup each)

1 large red bell pepper, finely chopped
1 medium tomato, chopped
2 cloves garlic, minced
1/4 to 1/2 teaspoon minced, seeded jalapeño pepper
1 tablespoon finely chopped fresh basil leaves, *or* 1 teaspoon dried
1 tablespoon finely chopped fresh cilantro leaves, *or* 1 teaspoon dried
2 teaspoons olive, *or* vegetable oil
2 teaspoons red wine vinegar
1/4 teaspoon salt
1/4 teaspoon pepper

1. Mix all ingredients; refrigerate 3 to 4 hours for flavors to blend.

Nutritional Data

PER SERVING		EXCHANGES	
Calories	182	Milk	0.0
% Calories from fat	20	Veg.	1.0
Fat (gm)	4	Fruit	0.0
Sat. Fat (gm)	0.7	Bread	1.5
Cholesterol (mg)	33.8	Meat	0.0
Sodium (mg)	215	Fat	1.0
Protein (gm)	6		
Carbohydrate (gm)	31		

PASTA WITH OYSTER MUSHROOMS

A wide variety of wild or exotic mushrooms are now readily available in supermarkets: oyster, shiitaki, enoki, cremini, morel, portobello, etc. Although this recipe specifies oyster mushrooms, feel free to substitute any other type.

6 Servings

8 ounces oyster mushrooms
2 to 3 teaspoons minced garlic
2 tablespoons margarine
1 tablespoon flour
1 cup skim milk
¼ cup low-salt chicken broth
1 teaspoon lemon juice
½ cup chopped, seeded tomato
¼ teaspoon salt
¼ teaspoon pepper
6 ounces fettuccine, cooked, warm
1 tablespoon grated Parmesan cheese

1. Separate oyster mushrooms into pieces. Saute mushrooms and garlic in margarine in large skillet until soft, about 5 minutes. Stir in flour; cook 1 minute.

2. Add milk, broth, and lemon juice to skillet; heat to boiling. Reduce heat and simmer, uncovered, until liquid is reduced by half. Stir in tomato, salt, and pepper; cook over medium heat until hot. Spoon sauce over pasta; sprinkle with Parmesan cheese.

Nutritional Data

PER SERVING		EXCHANGES	
Calories	164	Milk	0.0
% Calories from fat	30	Veg.	1.5
Fat (gm)	5.5	Fruit	0.0
Sat. Fat (gm)	1	Bread	1.0
Cholesterol (mg)	1.5	Meat	0.0
Sodium (mg)	227	Fat	1.0
Protein (gm)	7.5		
Carbohydrate (gm)	22.2		

ROASTED EGGPLANT WITH PASTA

Cook the eggplant on a charcoal grill to get a wonderful smoky flavor. The eggplant can be roasted or grilled up to 2 days in advance; refrigerate it in a plastic bag.

6 Servings

     1 medium eggplant (3/4 pound)
     1 large tomato, seeded, coarsely chopped
     4 green onions, sliced
     2 tablespoons balsamic vinegar, *or* red
        wine vinegar
     1 tablespoon olive oil
1 to 2 teaspoons lemon juice
     1 tablespoon finely chopped parsley
  1½ cups (6 ounces) fusilli or rotini (spirals or
        corkscrews), cooked, room temperature

1. Heat oven to 425° F. Pierce eggplant 6 to 8 times with fork; place in baking pan. Bake, uncovered, until tender, about 20 minutes. Cool until warm enough to handle easily. Cut eggplant in half; scoop out pulp with large spoon, and cut into 3/4-inch pieces.

2. Combine eggplant, tomato, and onions in bowl; stir in vinegar, oil, lemon juice, and parsley. Spoon over pasta and toss.

Nutritional Data

PER SERVING		EXCHANGES	
Calories	140	Milk	0.0
% Calories from fat	19	Veg.	1.5
Fat (gm)	3	Fruit	0.0
Sat. Fat (gm)	0.5	Bread	1.0
Cholesterol (mg)	0	Meat	0.0
Sodium (mg)	7	Fat	0.5
Protein (gm)	4.5		
Carbohydrate (gm)	24		

2
SOUPS

A s with most soups, flavors meld and improve if these recipes are
made at least a day in advance. Pasta absorbs broth and liquid in
storage, however, so additional broth may need to be added to thin
the consistency of thickened soups. Or make the soups without pasta in
advance, adding and cooking the pasta prior to serving. First-course soups
can, of course, be doubled in amount for entree servings.

CANNELLINI AND CABBAGE SOUP

Tuscany is known for its dishes with small, white cannellini beans. Cannellini beans are available in specialty sections of supermarkets or in Italian markets; canned great northern beans may be substituted.

4 Entree Servings (about 2 cups each)

Vegetable cooking spray
3 cups thinly sliced or chopped cabbage
1 small onion, coarsely chopped
3 cloves garlic, minced
1 teaspoon caraway seeds, crushed
2 cans (15 ounces each) low-salt chicken broth
1 cup water
1 can (15 ounces) cannellini, *or* great northern beans, rinsed, drained
1/2 cup (4 ounces) mostaccioli (penne), uncooked
1/4 teaspoon salt (optional)
1/4 teaspoon pepper

1. Spray large saucepan with cooking spray; heat over medium heat until hot. Saute cabbage, onions, garlic, and caraway seeds until cabbage begins to wilt, 8 to 10 minutes.

2. Add chicken broth, water, and beans to saucepan; heat to boiling. Stir in pasta; reduce heat and simmer, uncovered, until pasta is *al dente*, about 15 minutes. Stir in salt and pepper.

Nutritional Data

PER SERVING		EXCHANGES	
Calories	213	Milk	0.0
% Calories from fat	7	Veg.	2.0
Fat (gm)	1.9	Fruit	0.0
Sat. Fat (gm)	0.1	Bread	2.0
Cholesterol (mg)	0	Meat	0.5
Sodium (mg)	350	Fat	0.0
Protein (gm)	13.8		
Carbohydrate (gm)	43.7		

CHICKEN-VEGETABLE SOUP WITH ORZO

Escarole, which lends a unique taste to this hearty soup, is also a flavorful addition to green salads. Spinach leaves can be substituted for the escarole in this recipe, if desired.

4 Entree Servings *(about 2 cups each)*

Olive oil cooking spray
12 ounces boneless, skinless chicken breast, cut into $1/2$-inch pieces
1 medium onion, coarsely chopped
2 medium carrots, sliced
2 medium ribs celery, sliced
3 cloves garlic, minced
$1/2$ teaspoon dried thyme leaves
$1/2$ teaspoon dried oregano leaves
2 cans (15 ounces each) low-salt chicken broth
1 cup water
$1/2$ cup (4 ounces) orzo, uncooked
$1/2$ cup frozen peas
4 medium leaves escarole, sliced or coarsely chopped
$1/4$ teaspoon salt
$1/2$ teaspoon pepper
2 tablespoons grated Romano cheese

1. Spray large saucepan with cooking spray; heat over medium heat until hot. Cook chicken until no longer pink in center, about 8 minutes; remove from saucepan. Add onions, carrots, celery, and herbs to saucepan; saute until onion is tender, about 5 minutes. Return chicken to saucepan.

2. Add chicken broth and water to saucepan; heat to boiling. Stir in orzo, peas, and escarole. Reduce heat and simmer, uncovered, until orzo is *al dente*, about 7 minutes. Season with salt and pepper. Spoon soup into bowls; sprinkle with cheese.

Nutritional Data

PER SERVING		EXCHANGES	
Calories	260	Milk	0.0
% Calories from fat	15	Veg.	1.5
Fat (gm)	4.1	Fruit	0.0
Sat. Fat (gm)	1.3	Bread	1.5
Cholesterol (mg)	47.1	Meat	2.0
Sodium (mg)	281	Fat	0.0
Protein (gm)	24		
Carbohydrate (gm)	29.9		

ITALIAN MEATBALL SOUP

Flavorful meatballs for this soup are made with low-fat ground turkey rather than ground beef. Substitute other pastas for the spaghetti, if you like, such as orecchiette ("little ears") or conchiglie (shells).

8 Entree Servings (about 2 cups each)

1½ pounds ground turkey
2 egg whites
¼ cup Italian-seasoned breadcrumbs
4 cloves garlic, minced, divided
3 tablespoons Italian seasoning, divided
Olive oil cooking spray
4 cans (15 ounces each) low-salt chicken broth
3 cups water
2 cups green beans, diagonally cut into ½-inch pieces
4 medium carrots, sliced
2 medium onions, coarsely chopped
8 ounces thin spaghetti, uncooked, broken into 2 to 3-inch pieces
2 medium plum tomatoes, coarsely chopped

1. Mix ground turkey, egg whites, breadcrumbs, 2 cloves of garlic, and 1 tablespoon of Italian seasoning until well blended; shape mixture into 32 meatballs. Spray large skillet with cooking spray; heat over medium heat until hot. Cook meatballs until browned on all sides, 5 to 7 minutes; remove from heat and reserve.

2. Heat chicken broth, water, green beans, carrots, onions, remaining 2 cloves garlic, and remaining 1 tablespoon Italian seasoning to boiling in large saucepan; reduce heat and simmer, covered, until vegetables are almost tender, about 8 minutes.

3. Heat soup to boiling; add pasta and tomatoes. Reduce heat and simmer, uncovered, until pasta is *al dente,* about 10 minutes, adding meatballs during last 5 minutes. Serve immediately.

Nutritional Data

PER SERVING		EXCHANGES	
Calories	270	Milk	0.0
% Calories from fat	28	Veg.	1.0
Fat (gm)	8.7	Fruit	0.0
Sat. Fat (gm)	2	Bread	1.5
Cholesterol (mg)	31.7	Meat	2.0
Sodium (mg)	174	Fat	0.5
Protein (gm)	19		
Carbohydrate (gm)	30.2		

TWO-BEAN AND PASTA SOUP

◆

This substantial soup thickens upon standing; thin with additional chicken broth or water, if necessary.

6 Entree Servings (about 2 cups each)

Vegetable cooking spray
1½ cups cubed carrots
1 medium green bell pepper, chopped
½ cup sliced green onions and tops
3 cloves garlic, minced
2 teaspoons dried basil leaves
2 teaspoons dried oregano leaves
2 cans (15 ounces each) low-salt chicken broth
1 cup water
1 can (15 ounces) no-salt-added stewed tomatoes
1 can (15 ounces) cannellini, *or* great northern beans, rinsed, drained
1 can (15 ounces) fava beans, *or* pinto beans, rinsed, drained
1½ cups (4 ounces) rigatoni, uncooked
2 to 3 teaspoons lemon juice
¼ teaspoon salt
½ teaspoon pepper

1. Spray large saucepan with cooking spray; saute carrots, bell pepper, onions, and garlic until vegetables are tender, about 7 minutes. Stir in basil and oregano; cook 1 to 2 minutes.

2. Add chicken broth, water, tomatoes, and both beans to saucepan; heat to boiling. Reduce heat and simmer, covered, 10 minutes.

3. Heat soup to boiling; add pasta to saucepan. Reduce heat and simmer, uncovered, until pasta is *al dente,* 12 to 15 minutes. Season with lemon juice, salt, and pepper. Serve immediately.

Nutritional Data

PER SERVING		EXCHANGES	
Calories	222	Milk	0.0
% Calories from fat	7	Veg.	2.0
Fat (gm)	2	Fruit	0.0
Sat. Fat (gm)	0.1	Bread	2.0
Cholesterol (mg)	0	Meat	0.5
Sodium (mg)	534	Fat	0.0
Protein (gm)	14.3		
Carbohydrate (gm)	43.8		

SUN-DRIED TOMATO AND LINGUINE SOUP

♦

For this skinny pasta soup, be sure to use plain sun-dried tomatoes rather than the ones packed in oil. One-half cup of uncooked orzo can be substituted for the linguine, if preferred.

4 Side-Dish Servings *(about 1 cup each)*

   2 sun-dried tomatoes
      Hot water
      Vegetable cooking spray
 1/2 cup thinly sliced celery
   2 tablespoons thinly sliced green onions
      and tops
   2 cloves garlic, minced
   2 cans (15 ounces each) low-salt chicken broth
   2 ounces linguine, uncooked, broken into
      2 to 3-inch pieces
1 to 2 teaspoons lemon juice

1. Place tomatoes in small bowl; pour hot water over to cover. Let tomatoes stand until softened, about 15 minutes; drain. Coarsely chop tomatoes.

2. Spray medium saucepan with cooking spray; heat over medium heat until hot. Saute celery, onions, and garlic until tender, 5 to 7 minutes. Stir in chicken broth and tomatoes; heat to boiling.

3. Add linguine to boiling broth. Reduce heat and simmer, uncovered, until pasta is *al dente*, about 10 minutes. Season with lemon juice.

Nutritional Data

PER SERVING		EXCHANGES	
Calories	68	Milk	0.0
% Calories from fat	11	Veg.	1.0
Fat (gm)	0.9	Fruit	0.0
Sat. Fat (gm)	0	Bread	0.5
Cholesterol (mg)	0	Meat	0.0
Sodium (mg)	71	Fat	0.0
Protein (gm)	3.6		
Carbohydrate (gm)	12.1		

HERBED BROCCOLI AND PASTA SOUP

A wonderfully versatile soup, as any vegetable in season and any choice of herb can be substituted for the broccoli and thyme. For an entree soup, add 12 ounces of cubed cooked chicken breast (not included in Nutritional Data) during the last 10 minutes of cooking time.

6 Side-Dish Servings (about 1 cup each)

3 cans (15 ounces each) low-salt chicken broth
4 cloves garlic, minced
2 to 3 teaspoons dried thyme leaves
3 cups small broccoli florets
2¼ cups (6 ounces) fusilli (spirals), uncooked
2 to 3 tablespoons lemon juice
¼ teaspoon salt
⅛ teaspoon pepper

1. Heat chicken broth, garlic, and thyme to boiling in medium saucepan. Stir in broccoli and fusilli. Reduce heat and simmer, uncovered, until broccoli is tender and pasta is *al dente*, about 10 minutes.

2. Season soup with lemon juice, salt, and pepper. Serve immediately.

Nutritional Data

PER SERVING		EXCHANGES	
Calories	125	Milk	0.0
% Calories from fat	8	Veg.	0.5
Fat (gm)	1.1	Fruit	0.0
Sat. Fat (gm)	0.2	Bread	1.5
Cholesterol (mg)	0	Meat	0.0
Sodium (mg)	134	Fat	0.0
Protein (gm)	6.4		
Carbohydrate (gm)	23		

SPINACH AND TORTELLONI SOUP

Pasta soups can be made 2 to 3 days in advance, enhancing flavors. Add pasta to the soup when reheating for serving so that the pasta is fresh and perfectly cooked.

6 Side-Dish Servings (about 1 cup each)

Vegetable cooking spray
2 cups sliced carrots
1/4 cup sliced green onions and tops
2 cloves garlic, minced
1 teaspoon dried basil leaves
2 cans (15 ounces each) low-salt chicken broth
1 1/2 cups water
1 package (9 ounces) fresh low-fat tomato and cheese tortelloni
3 cups torn spinach leaves
2 to 3 teaspoons lemon juice
1/8 to 1/4 teaspoon ground nutmeg
1/8 teaspoon pepper

1. Spray bottom of large saucepan with cooking spray; heat over medium heat until hot. Saute carrots, onions, garlic, and basil until onions are tender, about 5 minutes.

2. Add chicken broth and water to saucepan; heat to boiling. Reduce heat and simmer, covered, 10 minutes.

3. Heat broth mixture to boiling; stir in tomato and cheese tortelloni and spinach. Reduce heat and simmer, uncovered, until tortelloni are *al dente*, about 5 minutes. Season with lemon juice, nutmeg, and pepper.

Nutritional Data

PER SERVING		EXCHANGES	
Calories	170	Milk	0.0
% Calories from fat	18	Veg.	1.0
Fat (gm)	3.5	Fruit	0.0
Sat. Fat (gm)	1.6	Bread	1.5
Cholesterol (mg)	17.7	Meat	0.0
Sodium (mg)	177	Fat	0.5
Protein (gm)	8.6		
Carbohydrate (gm)	26.9		

TORTELLONI AND MUSHROOM SOUP

Porcini mushrooms, an Italian delicacy found fresh in Tuscany in fall, are available in dried form year round. Porcini impart a wonderful "earthy" flavor to recipes. Dried mushrooms, such as shiitaki or Chinese black mushrooms, can be substituted for a similar flavor.

6 Side-Dish Servings (about 1 cup each)

2 ounces dried porcini mushrooms
  Hot water
  Vegetable cooking spray
8 ounces fresh white mushrooms, sliced
2 tablespoons finely chopped shallots, *or* green onions
2 cloves garlic, minced
1/2 teaspoon dried tarragon or thyme leaves
2 cans (15 ounces each) low-salt beef broth
1/4 cup dry sherry (optional)
1 package (9 ounces) fresh low-fat tomato and cheese tortelloni
1/4 teaspoon salt
1/4 teaspoon pepper

1. Place dried mushrooms in bowl; pour hot water over to cover. Let stand until mushrooms are soft, about 15 minutes; drain. Slice mushrooms, discarding any tough parts.

2. Spray large saucepan with cooking spray; heat over medium heat until hot. Saute dried and white mushrooms, shallots, garlic, and tarragon until mushrooms are tender, about 5 minutes.

3. Add beef broth and sherry to vegetables; heat to boiling. Add tomato and cheese tortelloni, salt, and pepper. Reduce heat and simmer, uncovered, until tortelloni are *al dente*, about 5 minutes.

Nutritional Data

PER SERVING		EXCHANGES	
Calories	188	Milk	0.0
% Calories from fat	19	Veg.	1.0
Fat (gm)	4.2	Fruit	0.0
Sat. Fat (gm)	1.5	Bread	1.5
Cholesterol (mg)	17.7	Meat	0.5
Sodium (mg)	235	Fat	0.5
Protein (gm)	10.1		
Carbohydrate (gm)	28.8		

CHICKPEA AND PASTA SOUP

Many fresh garden vegetables can be substituted for the zucchini and celery in this soup—carrots, cauliflower, broccoli florets, mushrooms, peas, and green beans are possible choices.

4 Entree Servings (about 1³/₄ cups each)

Olive oil cooking spray
1 small zucchini, cubed
2 ribs celery, thinly sliced
1 medium onion, chopped
3 to 4 cloves garlic, minced
1 teaspoon dried rosemary leaves
1 teaspoon dried thyme leaves
1/8 teaspoon dried crushed red pepper
1 can (15 ounces) low-salt chicken broth
1 can (15 ounces) no-salt-added stewed tomatoes
1 can (15 ounces) chickpeas, rinsed, drained
2 cups water
1 cup (4 ounces) farfalle (bow ties), uncooked
2 tablespoons finely chopped parsley
2 to 3 teaspoons lemon juice

1. Spray bottom of large saucepan with cooking spray. Saute zucchini, celery, onion, and garlic until zucchini is crisp-tender, about 8 minutes. Stir in herbs; cook 1 to 2 minutes.

2. Add chicken broth, tomatoes, chickpeas, and water; heat to boiling. Reduce heat and simmer, covered, 10 minutes.

3. Heat soup to boiling; add pasta to saucepan. Reduce heat and simmer, uncovered, until pasta is *al dente*, about 8 minutes. Stir in parsley; season with lemon juice.

Nutritional Data

PER SERVING		EXCHANGES	
Calories	259	Milk	0.0
% Calories from fat	7	Veg.	2.0
Fat (gm)	2.3	Fruit	0.0
Sat. Fat (gm)	0.2	Bread	2.5
Cholesterol (mg)	0	Meat	0.5
Sodium (mg)	224	Fat	0.0
Protein (gm)	15		
Carbohydrate (gm)	51.1		

SUMMER MINESTRONE

◆

Thick and savory, this traditional Italian soup is always a favorite.

8 Side-Dish Servings (about 1 cup each)

Vegetable cooking spray

2 medium potatoes, cubed

2 medium carrots, thinly sliced

1 small zucchini, cubed

1 cup halved green beans

1 cup thinly sliced or shredded cabbage

1/2 cup thinly sliced celery

1 medium onion, coarsely chopped

3 to 4 cloves garlic, minced

2 teaspoons Italian seasoning

1 to 2 teaspoons dried oregano leaves

2 cans (15 ounces) low-salt chicken broth

1 can (15 ounces) no-salt-added stewed tomatoes

1 can (15 ounces) kidney beans, rinsed, drained

2 cups water

1 1/2 cups (4 ounces) mostaccioli (penne), uncooked

1/2 teaspoon pepper

2 tablespoons grated Parmesan *or* Romano cheese

1. Spray bottom of large saucepan with cooking spray; heat over medium heat until hot. Saute fresh vegetables (next 8 ingredients) until crisp-tender, 10 to 12 minutes. Stir in Italian seasoning and oregano; cook 1 to 2 minutes more.

2. Add chicken broth, tomatoes, beans, and water; heat to boiling. Reduce heat and simmer, covered, 10 minutes.

3. Heat soup to boiling; add pasta to saucepan. Reduce heat and simmer, uncovered, until pasta is *al dente*, 10 to 12 minutes. Stir in pepper.

4. Spoon soup into bowls; sprinkle with cheese. Serve immediately.

Nutritional Data

PER SERVING		EXCHANGES	
Calories	177	Milk	0.0
% Calories from fat	9	Veg.	2.0
Fat (gm)	1.8	Fruit	0.0
Sat. Fat (gm)	0.6	Bread	1.5
Cholesterol (mg)	1.2	Meat	0.5
Sodium (mg)	256	Fat	0.0
Protein (gm)	8.1		
Carbohydrate (gm)	33.7		

3
SALADS

If making pasta salad in advance, do not add a vinaigrette dressing until serving time as the salad will absorb the dressing upon standing and become too dry in texture. Or, add the dressing to the salad ingredients without the pasta, and toss with the pasta just before serving.

Side-dish salads can be served as a first course; they can also be doubled to serve as an entree.

WARM PAPPARDELLE SALAD WITH CAJUN SHRIMP

Pappardelle is a very wide pasta, measuring about 1 inch in width. Any of the wide, flat pastas, such as mafalde or trenette, are also appropriate for this highly spiced dish.

4 Entree Servings

Olive oil cooking spray
1/2 medium red bell pepper, sliced
1/4 cup onions, sliced
2 teaspoons dried oregano leaves
2 teaspoons dried basil leaves
2 teaspoons dried thyme leaves
1/2 teaspoon garlic powder
1/2 teaspoon paprika
1/4 teaspoon cayenne pepper
1/4 teaspoon black pepper
1/4 teaspoon salt
12 ounces peeled, deveined shrimp
1 cup low-salt chicken broth
1/4 cup dry white wine, *or* low-salt chicken broth
1 tablespoon tomato paste
8 ounces pappardelle pasta, cooked, warm

1. Spray large skillet with cooking spray; heat over medium heat until hot. Saute bell pepper and onions until tender. Stir in herbs, garlic powder, paprika, cayenne, black pepper, and salt.

2. Add shrimp to skillet; cook over medium heat until shrimp just begin to turn pink. Stir in broth, wine, and tomato paste; heat to boiling. Reduce heat and simmer 15 minutes. Serve over pasta.

Nutritional Data

PER SERVING		EXCHANGES	
Calories	292	Milk	0.0
% Calories from fat	7	Veg.	0.5
Fat (gm)	2.2	Fruit	0.0
Sat. Fat (gm)	0.5	Bread	3.0
Cholesterol (mg)	130.6	Meat	1.0
Sodium (mg)	329	Fat	0.0
Protein (gm)	22.7		
Carbohydrate (gm)	41.4		

SESAME PASTA WITH SUMMER VEGETABLES

———————◆———————

These garden vegetables signal the end of summer harvest. The vegetables used in this salad can vary according to seasonal availability.

6 Side-Dish Servings

 1 small eggplant
 1 cup sliced carrots, steamed until crisp-tender
 1 cup sliced summer yellow squash, steamed until crisp-tender
 1 cup broccoli florets, steamed until crisp-tender
 1 medium red bell pepper, sliced
 1/4 cup sliced green onions and tops
   Sesame Dressing (recipe follows)
 8 ounces thin spaghetti, cooked, room temperature
 2 teaspoons toasted sesame seeds

1. Heat oven to 400° F. Pierce eggplant 6 to 8 times with fork; place in baking pan. Bake, uncovered, until tender, about 20 minutes. Cool until warm enough to handle easily. Cut eggplant in half; scoop out pulp with a large spoon and cut into 3/4-inch pieces.

2. Combine eggplant and remaining vegetables in bowl; pour Sesame Dressing over and toss. Add pasta and toss; sprinkle with sesame seeds.

Sesame Dressing

Makes about 1/3 cup

 2 tablespoons reduced-sodium soy sauce
 2 tablespoons sesame oil
 1 teaspoon hot chili oil (optional)
 1 tablespoon balsamic, *or* red wine vinegar
 1 1/2 tablespoons sugar
 1 clove garlic, minced
 1 tablespoon finely chopped cilantro, *or* parsley

1. Mix all ingredients; refrigerate until serving time. Mix again before using.

Nutritional Data

PER SERVING		EXCHANGES	
Calories	192	Milk	0.0
% Calories from fat	30	Veg.	1.5
Fat (gm)	6.6	Fruit	0.0
Sat. Fat (gm)	0.7	Bread	1.5
Cholesterol (mg)	0	Meat	0.0
Sodium (mg)	428	Fat	1.0
Protein (gm)	7.2		
Carbohydrate (gm)	28.3		

MIXED VEGETABLES AND ORZO VINAIGRETTE

The spice turmeric, used in the salad dressing, gives this salad its unusual yellow color. Curry powder can be used instead, imparting the same color but adding a delicate curry flavor.

8 Side-Dish Servings

2 medium zucchini, thinly sliced

8 ounces asparagus, cut into 1½-inch pieces, steamed

1 cup frozen, thawed peas

½ cup sliced carrots, steamed

¾ cup (6 ounces) orzo, cooked

Mustard-Turmeric Vinaigrette (recipe follows)

2 cups torn lettuce leaves

4 cherry tomatoes, cut into halves

1. Combine zucchini, asparagus, peas, carrots, and orzo in bowl; pour Mustard-Turmeric Vinaigrette over and toss. Spoon onto lettuce on salad plates; garnish with tomatoes.

Mustard-Turmeric Vinaigrette

Makes about ½ cup

¼ cup red wine vinegar

¼ teaspoon ground turmeric

2 to 3 tablespoons lemon juice

2 tablespoons olive, *or* vegetable oil

2 teaspoons Dijon-style mustard

2 cloves garlic, minced
¼ teaspoon salt
¼ teaspoon pepper

1. Heat vinegar and turmeric in small saucepan over medium heat until turmeric is dissolved, stirring constantly, 2 to 3 minutes; cool.

2. Combine vinegar mixture and remaining ingredients; refrigerate until serving time. Mix again before using.

Nutritional Data

PER SERVING		EXCHANGES	
Calories	142	Milk	0.0
% Calories from fat	27	Veg.	1.0
Fat (gm)	4.2	Fruit	0.0
Sat. Fat (gm)	0.6	Bread	1.0
Cholesterol (mg)	0	Meat	0.0
Sodium (mg)	112	Fat	1.0
Protein (gm)	5.5		
Carbohydrate (gm)	20.9		

GARDEN VEGETABLE AND PASTA SALAD

Steaming is a healthful, fat-free method of cooking vegetables. Steam broccoli and cauliflower florets just until crisp-tender for this delicious, meatless entree.

4 Entree Servings

 1 medium eggplant, cut into 1/2-inch slices
   Vegetable cooking spray
 2 cups cauliflower florets, steamed, cooled
 2 cups broccoli florets, steamed, cooled
10 cherry tomatoes
 1/2 medium green bell pepper, sliced
 8 ounces fettuccine, *or* linguine, cooked, room
   temperature
   Basil Vinaigrette (recipe follows)
 2 ounces feta cheese, crumbled

1. Heat oven to 400° F. Spray both sides of eggplant with cooking spray; arrange on cookie sheet. Bake until eggplant is tender, about 15 minutes. Cool. Cut into 1/2-inch pieces.

2. Combine eggplant, remaining vegetables, and linguine in large bowl; pour Basil Vinaigrette over and toss. Sprinkle with cheese.

Basil Vinaigrette

Makes about 1/3 cup

 1/4 cup balsamic vinegar
 1 tablespoon olive oil
 2 tablespoons finely chopped fresh basil leaves,
   or 2 teaspoons dried
 2 tablespoons finely chopped parsley
 1/4 teaspoon salt
 1/4 teaspoon pepper

1. Mix all ingredients; refrigerate until serving time. Stir before using.

Nutritional Data

PER SERVING		EXCHANGES	
Calories	304	Milk	0.0
% Calories from fat	25	Veg.	2.0
Fat (gm)	9	Fruit	0.0
Sat. Fat (gm)	2.7	Bread	2.5
Cholesterol (mg)	12.5	Meat	0.0
Sodium (mg)	423	Fat	1.5
Protein (gm)	12.8		
Carbohydrate (gm)	47.2		

TORTELLONI SALAD WITH CHICKEN AND MINTED PESTO

The Mint Pesto provides a refreshing flavor counterpoint to chicken and pasta.

6 Servings

Olive oil cooking spray

12 ounces boneless, skinless chicken breast, cut diagonally into 1/2-inch slices

1/4 cup finely chopped shallots, *or* onions

3 green onions and tops, sliced

2 cloves garlic, minced

1/2 cup dry white wine, *or* low-salt chicken broth

2 tablespoons lemon juice

3/4 cup **Minted Pesto** (3/4 recipe, see pg. 85)

1 1/2 packages (9-ounce size) mushroom-cheese tortelloni, cooked

1/2 cup sliced yellow bell pepper

1/2 cup sliced red bell pepper

Lettuce leaves, as garnish

6 cherry tomatoes, halved

Mint sprigs, as garnish

1. Spray medium skillet with cooking spray; heat over medium heat until hot. Saute chicken until browned and no longer pink in the center, about 8 minutes. Remove chicken and reserve.

2. Add shallots, green onions, and garlic to skillet; saute until tender, 3 to 5 minutes. Add wine and lemon juice; heat to boiling. Add chicken and simmer, uncovered, until liquid has evaporated, 8 to 10 minutes.

3. Spoon Minted Pesto over tortelloni and toss; add chicken mixture and bell peppers and toss. Refrigerate to chill lightly, about 1 hour.

4. Spoon salad onto lettuce-lined plates; garnish with cherry tomatoes and mint.

Nutritional Data

PER SERVING		EXCHANGES	
Calories	292	Milk	0.0
% Calories from fat	31	Veg.	1.0
Fat (gm)	10.7	Fruit	0.0
Sat. fat (gm)	3.2	Bread	1.5
Cholesterol (mg)	57	Meat	2.0
Sodium (mg)	212	Fat	1.0
Protein (gm)	21.6		
Carbohydrate (gm)	28		

"LITTLE EARS" WITH SHRIMP AND VEGETABLES

For variety, cooked cubed chicken breast, lean beef, or lean pork can be substituted for the shrimp in this entree salad.

4 Entree Servings

12 ounces peeled, deveined shrimp, cooked
3 cups broccoli florets, steamed
1 medium yellow or green bell pepper, sliced
12 cherry tomatoes, cut into halves
2 cups (8 ounces) "little ears," *or* small pasta
   shells, cooked
   Mustard Seed Vinaigrette (recipe follows)

1. Combine shrimp, vegetables, and pasta in serving bowl; pour Mustard Seed Vinaigrette over and toss.

Mustard Seed Vinaigrette

Makes about 1/3 cup

2 tablespoons olive oil
2 tablespoons white wine vinegar
2 tablespoons lemon juice
2 medium shallots, finely chopped
2 cloves garlic, finely chopped
2 tablespoons finely chopped cilantro, *or* parsley
1/2 teaspoon mustard seed, crushed
1/2 teaspoon salt
1/4 teaspoon pepper

1. Mix all ingredients; refrigerate until serving time. Stir before using.

Nutritional Data

PER SERVING		EXCHANGES	
Calories	367	Milk	0.0
% Calories from fat	23	Veg.	2.0
Fat (gm)	9.6	Fruit	0.0
Sat. Fat (gm)	1.4	Bread	2.5
Cholesterol (mg)	130.6	Meat	2.0
Sodium (mg)	451	Fat	0.5
Protein (gm)	24.7		
Carbohydrate (gm)	47.3		

Angel Hair Salad

Goat's cheese adds a creamy texture and piquant accent to this flavorful pasta dish.

4 Entree Servings

Vegetable cooking spray
8 ounces snow peas
8 ounces mushrooms, sliced
3 medium carrots, cut into julienne pieces
4 large plum tomatoes, sliced
2 teaspoons dried oregano leaves
1 teaspoon dried tarragon leaves
½ cup canned low-salt chicken broth
½ cup skim milk
2 teaspoons tomato paste
¼ teaspoon salt
¼ teaspoon pepper
3 ounces goat's cheese, *or* reduced-fat cream cheese
12 ounces capellini (angel hair), *or* thin spaghetti, cooked, warm

1. Spray large skillet with cooking spray; heat over medium heat until hot. Saute vegetables until snow peas are crisp-tender, 6 to 8 minutes. Stir in herbs; cook 1 minute.

2. Stir in chicken broth, milk, and tomato paste; heat to boiling. Reduce heat and simmer, uncovered, until thickened to sauce consistency, about 10 minutes, stirring occasionally. Stir in salt and pepper.

3. Stir goat's cheese into warm pasta until melted; add vegetable mixture and toss.

Nutritional Data

PER SERVING		EXCHANGES	
Calories	440	Milk	0.0
% Calories from fat	13	Veg.	4.0
Fat (gm)	6.5	Fruit	0.0
Sat. Fat (gm)	3.7	Bread	4.0
Cholesterol (mg)	19.4	Meat	0.0
Sodium (mg)	285	Fat	1.0
Protein (gm)	19.8		
Carbohydrate (gm)	76.1		

FUSILLI WITH FRESH TOMATOES AND CORN

A perfect salad, especially when homegrown tomatoes, corn, and basil are available!

8 Side-Dish Servings

2 cups plum tomatoes, chopped
1 cup fresh whole-kernel corn, cooked
1/2 cup sliced green onions and tops
2 2/3 cups (6 ounces) fusilli (spirals), *or* corkscrews, cooked, room temperature
Fresh Basil Dressing (recipe follows)

1. Combine tomatoes, corn, onions, and pasta in salad bowl; pour Fresh Basil Dressing over and toss.

Fresh Basil Dressing

Makes about 1/4 cup

1/3 cup red wine vinegar
2 tablespoons olive oil, *or* vegetable oil
3 tablespoons finely chopped fresh basil leaves, or 1 teaspoon dried
2 cloves garlic, minced
1/2 teaspoon salt
1/4 teaspoon pepper

1. Mix all ingredients; refrigerate until serving time. Stir before using.

Nutritional Data

PER SERVING		EXCHANGES	
Calories	135	Milk	0.0
% Calories from fat	26	Veg.	1.0
Fat (gm)	4	Fruit	0.0
Sat. Fat (gm)	0.6	Bread	1.0
Cholesterol (mg)	0	Meat	0.0
Sodium (mg)	141	Fat	1.0
Protein (gm)	4.1		
Carbohydrate (gm)	21.8		

BEEF AND PASTA SALAD VINAIGRETTE

Any lean beef or pork can be substituted for the flank steak. Slice meat diagonally, across the grain, into thin slices to maximize tenderness.

4 Entree Servings

12 ounces beef flank steak, excess fat trimmed, broiled or grilled to medium doneness, thinly sliced across grain

2 medium tomatoes, cut into wedges

1 medium yellow squash, *or* zucchini, diagonally sliced

1 medium green bell pepper, sliced

1 large carrot, diagonally sliced

1 small red onion, sliced

3 cups (8 ounces) rotini (corkscrews), cooked, room temperature

Mixed Herb Vinaigrette (recipe follows)

Lettuce leaves

1. Combine flank steak, tomatoes, squash, bell pepper, carrot, onions, and pasta in shallow glass baking dish. Pour Mixed Herb Vinaigrette over and toss. Refrigerate 1 to 2 hours for flavors to blend.

2. Arrange lettuce on salad plates; spoon salad over.

Mixed Herb Vinaigrette

Makes about ²/₃ cup

1/3 cup red wine vinegar

1/4 cup reduced-sodium beef broth, *or* water

1 tablespoon olive oil, *or* vegetable oil

2 teaspoons sugar

2 teaspoons Dijon-style mustard

1 teaspoon mustard seed, crushed

3 cloves garlic, minced

1 tablespoon finely chopped fresh marjoram leaves, *or* 1 teaspoon dried

1 tablespoon finely chopped fresh tarragon leaves, *or* 1 teaspoon dried

1 tablespoon finely chopped fresh thyme leaves, *or* 1/2 teaspoon dried

¹/₂ teaspoon salt
¹/₂ teaspoon pepper

1. Mix all ingredients; refrigerate until ready to use. Stir before using.

Nutritional Data

PER SERVING		EXCHANGES	
Calories	469	Milk	0.0
% Calories from fat	27	Veg.	2.0
Fat (gm)	14	Fruit	0.0
Sat. Fat (gm)	4.5	Bread	2.5
Cholesterol (mg)	57	Meat	0.0
Sodium (mg)	391	Fat	1.5
Protein (gm)	32.9		
Carbohydrate (gm)	52.1		

CHILI-DRESSED SALAD WITH RADIATORE

A fun pasta, radiatore look like the tiny radiators for which they are named! Other shaped pastas can be used, if preferred.

4 Entree Servings

Chili Dressing (recipe follows)
3 cups (8 ounces) radiatore (radiators), cooked, room temperature
1 can (9¹/₄ ounces) white tuna in water, drained, chunked
2 medium tomatoes, cut into wedges
¹/₂ medium avocado, peeled, pitted, cut into ³/₄-inch pieces
2 tablespoons finely chopped cilantro, *or* parsley
2 cups torn salad greens

1. Pour dressing over pasta in medium bowl and toss. Add tuna, tomatoes, avocado, and cilantro; toss. Spoon salad over greens on serving plate.

Chili Dressing

Makes about ¹/₄ cup

3 tablespoons lemon juice
2 tablespoons olive oil

½ teaspoon chili powder
¼ teaspoon crushed red pepper

1. Mix all ingredients; refrigerate until serving time. Mix again before using.

Nutritional Data

PER SERVING		EXCHANGES	
Calories	388	Milk	0.0
% Calories from fat	30	Veg.	2.0
Fat (gm)	12.9	Fruit	0.0
Sat. Fat (gm)	1.9	Bread	2.5
Cholesterol (mg)	18.7	Meat	2.0
Sodium (mg)	238	Fat	1.0
Protein (gm)	25.5		
Carbohydrate (gm)	43.2		

FETTUCCINE WITH ROASTED GARLIC, ONIONS, AND PEPPERS

◆

A salad that is deceptively simple to make, incredibly delicious to eat.

8 Side-Dish Servings

2 bulbs garlic
  Olive oil cooking spray
3 medium onions, cut into wedges
2 large red bell peppers, cut into ½-inch slices
2 tablespoons olive oil, *or* vegetable oil
2 tablespoons lemon juice
2 tablespoons finely chopped parsley
½ teaspoon salt
¼ teaspoon pepper
8 ounces fettuccine, cooked, warm

1. Heat oven to 400° F. Cut a scant ½ inch off tops of garlic bulbs, exposing ends of cloves. Wrap garlic heads loosely in aluminum foil. Spray jelly roll pan with cooking spray. Arrange garlic, onions, and bell peppers on pan. Bake vegetables, uncovered, until garlic is very soft and vegetables are tender, 15 to 20 minutes.

2. Cool garlic slightly; squeeze pulp into small bowl. Stir in oil, lemon juice, parsley, salt, and pepper. Spoon garlic mixture over pasta and toss; add onions and peppers and toss. Serve warm.

Nutritional Data

PER SERVING		EXCHANGES	
Calories	151	Milk	0.0
% Calories from fat	26	Veg.	1.5
Fat (gm)	4.5	Fruit	0.0
Sat. Fat (gm)	0.5	Bread	1.0
Cholesterol (mg)	0	Meat	0.0
Sodium (mg)	184	Fat	1.0
Protein (gm)	5		
Carbohydrate (gm)	24.4		

CURRIED PASTA SALAD

Especially delicious using flavored specialty pastas, such as curry, sesame, or tomato.

4 Servings

 ⅓ cup chopped mango chutney
 ¼ cup chopped mixed dried fruit
  2 tablespoons Dijon-style mustard
  1 tablespoon olive oil
  1 tablespoon lime juice
  8 ounces curry flavor, *or* plain, fettuccine, cooked
  1 cup frozen stir-fry-blend vegetables, cooked, cooled to room temperature
    Salt, cayenne, and black pepper, to taste
 ¼ cup sliced green onions and tops
2 to 4 tablespoons chopped cashews

1. Combine chutney, dried fruit, mustard, oil, and lime juice; spoon over fettuccine and toss. Add vegetables and toss; season to taste with salt and pepper.

2. Spoon pasta onto serving platter; sprinkle with green onions and cashews.

Nutritional Data

PER SERVING		EXCHANGES	
Calories	321	Milk	0.0
% Calories from fat	22	Veg.	0.0
Fat (gm)	8.1	Fruit	1.5
Sat. fat (gm)	0.9	Bread	2.5
Cholesterol (mg)	0	Meat	0.0
Sodium (mg)	207	Fat	1.5
Protein (gm)	9.3		
Carbohydrate (gm)	55.1		

PASTA, WHITE BEAN, AND RED CABBAGE SALAD

A hearty salad with a caraway accent. The salad can be made in advance, but stir in the cabbage just before serving for fresh color.

6 Side-Dish Servings

2¼ cups (6 ounces) rotini (corkscrews), cooked, room temperature

1 cup coarsely chopped or sliced red cabbage

1 cup canned, drained great northern beans

½ small onion, chopped

½ small red bell pepper, chopped

Caraway Dressing (recipe follows)

1. Combine pasta, cabbage, beans, onions, and bell pepper in bowl; stir in Caraway Dressing.

Caraway Dressing

Makes about 1 cup

½ cup fat-free mayonnaise, *or* salad dressing

½ cup fat-free sour cream

2 teaspoons lemon juice

2 cloves garlic, minced

1 teaspoon caraway seeds, crushed

¼ teaspoon salt (optional)

¼ teaspoon pepper

1. Mix all ingredients.

Nutritional Data

PER SERVING		EXCHANGES	
Calories	185	Milk	0.0
% Calories from fat	5	Veg.	1.5
Fat (gm)	1.1	Fruit	0.0
Sat. Fat (gm)	0.2	Bread	2.0
Cholesterol (mg)	0	Meat	0.0
Sodium (mg)	268	Fat	0.0
Protein (gm)	8.7		
Carbohydrate (gm)	35.9		

PASTA COLESLAW

The addition of pasta updates a traditional cabbage slaw.

4 Side-Dish Servings

1½ cups (4 ounces) fusilli (spirals), *or* farfalle
  (bow ties), cooked, room temperature
1 cup thinly sliced green cabbage
1 medium tomato, chopped
1 medium green bell pepper, chopped
¼ cup sliced celery
"Creamy" Dressing (recipe follows)

1. Combine pasta, cabbage, tomato, bell pepper, and celery in bowl; stir in "Creamy" Dressing.

"Creamy" Dressing

Makes about ½ cup

¼ cup fat-free mayonnaise, *or* salad dressing
¼ cup low-fat plain yogurt
1 tablespoon lemon juice
2 cloves garlic, minced
½ teaspoon dried tarragon leaves
¼ teaspoon salt (optional)
¼ teaspoon pepper

1. Mix all ingredients.

Nutritional Data

PER SERVING		EXCHANGES	
Calories	139	Milk	0.0
% Calories from fat	8	Veg.	1.0
Fat (gm)	1.2	Fruit	0.0
Sat. Fat (gm)	0.3	Bread	1.5
Cholesterol (mg)	0.9	Meat	0.0
Sodium (mg)	156	Fat	0.0
Protein (gm)	5.4		
Carbohydrate (gm)	27.3		

MACARONI-BLUE CHEESE SALAD

A not-so-traditional macaroni salad with blue cheese pizazz!

8 Side-Dish Servings

1 cup (4 ounces) elbow macaroni, cooked, room temperature
3/4 cup chopped red bell pepper
1/2 cup chopped cucumber
1/2 cup shredded carrots
1/4 cup thinly sliced green onions and tops
Blue Cheese Dressing (recipe follows)

1. Combine macaroni, bell pepper, cucumber, carrots, and green onions in bowl; stir in Blue Cheese Dressing.

Blue Cheese Dressing

Makes about 1/2 cup

1/2 cup fat-free mayonnaise, or salad dressing
2 tablespoons crumbled blue cheese
1 tablespoon red wine vinegar
1 teaspoon celery seeds
1/2 teaspoon salt (optional)
1/8 teaspoon cayenne pepper
1/8 teaspoon black pepper

1. Mix all ingredients; refrigerate until serving time. Mix again before using.

Nutritional Data

PER SERVING		EXCHANGES	
Calories	82	Milk	0.0
% Calories from fat	9	Veg.	2.0
Fat (gm)	0.9	Fruit	0.0
Sat. Fat (gm)	0.4	Bread	0.5
Cholesterol (mg)	1.3	Meat	0.0
Sodium (mg)	159	Fat	0.0
Protein (gm)	2.6		
Carbohydrate (gm)	16.3		

LIGHT SUMMER PASTA

The fragrant aroma and flavor of fresh herbs and garlic accents summer ripe tomatoes in this salad.

6 Side-Dish Servings

8 ounces spaghetti, cooked, room temperature
1 pound plum tomatoes, seeded, chopped
³/₄ cup (3 ounces) cubed (¹/₄ inch) reduced-fat mozzarella cheese
3 tablespoons finely chopped fresh basil leaves, *or* 2 teaspoons dried
2 tablespoons finely chopped parsley
Garlic Vinaigrette (recipe follows)

1. Combine spaghetti, tomatoes, cheese, and herbs in salad bowl; pour Garlic Vinaigrette over and toss.

Garlic Vinaigrette

Makes about ¹/₃ cup

3 tablespoons red wine vinegar
2 tablespoons olive oil
3 cloves garlic, minced
¹/₄ teaspoon salt
¹/₈ teaspoon pepper

1. Mix all ingredients; refrigerate until serving time. Mix again before using.

Nutritional Data

PER SERVING		EXCHANGES	
Calories	200	Milk	0.0
% Calories from fat	30	Veg.	1.0
Fat (gm)	7.6	Fruit	0.0
Sat. Fat (gm)	0.6	Bread	1.5
Cholesterol (mg)	5	Meat	0.0
Sodium (mg)	234	Fat	1.5
Protein (gm)	9.8		
Carbohydrate (gm)	26.2		

BRUSSELS SPROUTS AND GNOCCHI SALAD

Enjoy the first fall harvest of Brussels sprouts in this colorful salad. Pasta shells can be substituted for the gnocchi, if preferred.

8 Side-Dish Servings

2   cups (8 ounces) gnocchi, cooked, room temperature
8   ounces Brussels sprouts, cut into halves, steamed, cooled
1   cup seeded, chopped tomato
1   medium purple *or* green bell pepper, sliced
1/4 cup thinly sliced red onions
    Sun-Dried Tomato and Goat's Cheese Dressing (recipe follows)
2   tablespoons grated Romano cheese

1. Combine gnocchi and vegetables in salad bowl. Pour Sun-Dried Tomato and Goat's Cheese Dressing over salad and toss; sprinkle with grated cheese.

Sun-Dried Tomato and Goat's Cheese Dressing

Makes about 1/2 cup

3   sun-dried tomatoes
    Hot water
2   tablespoons olive oil
2   tablespoons white wine vinegar
2   tablespoons lemon juice

    1 tablespoon goat's cheese, *or* reduced-fat cream
       cheese, room temperature
    2 cloves garlic, minced
    1/2 teaspoon dried marjoram leaves
    1/8 teaspoon dried thyme leaves
    1/4 teaspoon salt
    1/8 teaspoon pepper

1. Place tomatoes in small bowl; pour hot water over to cover. Let tomatoes stand until softened, about 15 minutes; drain and finely chop.

2. Mix tomatoes, oil, and remaining ingredients; refrigerate until serving time. Mix again before using.

Nutritional Data

PER SERVING		EXCHANGES	
Calories	172	Milk	0.0
% Calories from fat	27	Veg.	1.0
Fat (gm)	5.4	Fruit	0.0
Sat. Fat (gm)	0.9	Bread	1.5
Cholesterol (mg)	3.5	Meat	0.0
Sodium (mg)	179	Fat	1.0
Protein (gm)	6.3		
Carbohydrate (gm)	26.3		

ORZO WITH SUN-DRIED TOMATOES AND MUSHROOMS

A simple salad, but intensely flavored with sun-dried tomatoes, fresh rosemary, and sherry. If desired, the sherry can be omitted.

4 Side-Dish Servings

- 2 sun-dried tomatoes (not in oil)
- Hot water
- Olive oil cooking spray
- 1½ cups sliced mushrooms
- ¼ cup thinly sliced green onions and tops
- 2 cloves garlic, minced
- ½ cup low-salt chicken broth
- 2 tablespoons dry sherry (optional)
- ½ cup (4 ounces) orzo, cooked, room temperature
- 2 tablespoons finely chopped fresh rosemary leaves, *or* 1 teaspoon dried
- 2 tablespoons finely chopped parsley
- ¼ teaspoon salt
- ¼ teaspoon pepper

1. Place tomatoes in small bowl; pour hot water over to cover. Let tomatoes stand until softened, about 15 minutes; drain and slice.

2. Spray large skillet with cooking spray; heat over medium heat until hot. Saute mushrooms, green onions, and garlic until mushrooms are tender, 5 to 7 minutes.

3. Add chicken broth, sherry, and tomatoes to skillet; heat to boiling. Reduce heat and simmer, uncovered, until liquid is reduced by half, about 5 minutes. Cool to room temperature.

4. Combine orzo and mushroom mixture in bowl; add remaining ingredients and toss.

Nutritional Data

PER SERVING		EXCHANGES	
Calories	122	Milk	0.0
% Calories from fat	8	Veg.	0.5
Fat (gm)	1.2	Fruit	0.0
Sat. Fat (gm)	0.2	Bread	1.5
Cholesterol (mg)	0	Meat	0.0
Sodium (mg)	239	Fat	0.0
Protein (gm)	5.4		
Carbohydrate (gm)	23.5		

SMOKED CHICKEN BREAST AND LINGUINE SALAD

Mesquite and hickory chips are most commonly used for smoking foods on the grill. For subtle flavor, try pecan, cherry, or alder wood when smoking the chicken for this salad. Mesquite-smoked chicken or turkey breast is also available in the deli sections of supermarkets.

4 Entree Servings

- 1 pound boneless, skinless chicken breasts
- 8 ounces linguine, cooked, room temperature
- 2 cups sliced carrots, steamed until crisp-tender
- 1/2 can (15-ounce size) artichoke hearts, drained, rinsed, cut into fourths
- 12 cherry tomatoes, cut into halves
- 1/4 cup sliced green onions and tops
  Sour Cream Dressing (recipe follows)

1. Smoke chicken in smoker or on grill, using manufacturer's directions. Cool; refrigerate several hours or overnight to allow flavor to mellow. Cut chicken into strips or pieces.

2. Combine pasta, chicken, and vegetables in bowl; spoon Sour Cream Dressing over and toss.

Sour Cream Dressing

Makes about 2/3 cup

- 1/3 cup fat-free sour cream
- 1/3 cup fat-free mayonnaise, *or* salad dressing

    1 tablespoon red wine vinegar
    1 clove garlic, minced
    1/2 teaspoon dried rosemary leaves, crushed
    1/2 teaspoon salt
    1/4 teaspoon pepper

1. Mix all ingredients; refrigerate until serving time. Mix again before using.

Nutritional Data

PER SERVING		EXCHANGES	
Calories	404	Milk	0.0
% Calories from fat	11	Veg.	4.0
Fat (gm)	5.2	Fruit	0.0
Sat. Fat (gm)	0.8	Bread	2.5
Cholesterol (mg)	58	Meat	2.0
Sodium (mg)	800	Fat	0.0
Protein (gm)	34.9		
Carbohydrate (gm)	58.5		

TUNA, FENNEL, AND PASTA SALAD WITH ORANGE VINAIGRETTE

◆

Use fresh fish if at all possible; haddock, halibut, or salmon are alternatives to the tuna. The orange segments and fennel are fresh flavor counterpoints to the fish.

6 Entree Servings

- 1 pound tuna steaks, grilled or broiled, warm
- 1½ cups (6 ounces) conchiglie (shells), cooked, room temperature
- 3 cups torn leaf lettuce
- 2 medium heads Belgium endive, torn into bite-size pieces
- 2 oranges, cut into segments
- ½ cup very thinly sliced fennel bulb, *or* celery
- 1 small red bell pepper, sliced

  Orange Vinaigrette (recipe follows)

1. Remove skin and any bones from fish and discard; break fish into large chunks.

2. Combine pasta shells, greens, orange segments, fennel, and bell pepper in salad bowl. Pour Orange Vinaigrette over and toss. Add warm fish and toss.

Orange Vinaigrette

Makes about ⅔ cup

- ¼ cup orange juice
- 3 tablespoons olive oil
- 3 tablespoons balsamic vinegar, *or* red wine vinegar
- 2 tablespoons finely chopped shallots, *or* red onions
- 2 cloves garlic, minced
- 1 teaspoon dried rosemary leaves
- ½ teaspoon fennel seeds, crushed
- ¼ teaspoon salt
- ⅛ teaspoon ground white pepper

1. Mix all ingredients; refrigerate until serving time. Mix again before using.

Nutritional Data

PER SERVING		EXCHANGES	
Calories	296	Milk	0.0
% Calories from fat	26	Veg.	1.0
Fat (gm)	8.6	Fruit	0.5
Sat. Fat (gm)	1.2	Bread	1.5
Cholesterol (mg)	33.9	Meat	2.0
Sodium (mg)	140	Fat	0.5
Protein (gm)	23.4		
Carbohydrate (gm)	31.6		

PASTA AND CRAB MEAT SALAD WITH FRUIT VINAIGRETTE

Any firm-textured fish, such as halibut or haddock, can be substituted for the crab meat; surimi can also be used.

4 Entree Servings

6 ounces crab meat, flaked into ½-inch pieces
1 small cucumber, peeled, seeded, chopped
1 medium tomato, seeded, chopped
1 cup cooked peas
8 ounces farfalle (bow ties), cooked, room temperature
Fruit Vinaigrette (recipe follows)

1. Combine crab meat, cucumber, tomato, peas, and pasta in salad bowl. Pour Fruit Vinaigrette over and toss.

Fruit Vinaigrette

Makes about ⅔ cup

¼ cup orange juice
3 tablespoons raspberry red wine vinegar
2 tablespoons lime juice
1 tablespoon olive oil
1 clove garlic, minced
2 tablespoons finely chopped cilantro, *or* tarragon, *or* parsley
1 teaspoon grated lime rind
¼ teaspoon ground nutmeg
¼ teaspoon salt

¹/₈ teaspoon cayenne pepper
¹/₈ teaspoon ground black pepper

1. Mix all ingredients; refrigerate until serving time. Mix again before using.

Nutritional Data

PER SERVING		EXCHANGES	
Calories	330	Milk	0.0
% Calories from fat	16	Veg.	1.0
Fat (gm)	6.1	Fruit	0.0
Sat. Fat (gm)	0.9	Bread	3.0
Cholesterol (mg)	42.5	Meat	1.0
Sodium (mg)	267	Fat	0.5
Protein (gm)	19.4		
Carbohydrate (gm)	50.1		

ROAST PORK AND APPLE SALAD WITH PASTA

Roast pork tenderloin can be warm or at room temperature when tossed with the salad; apples can be sweet or tart, as preferred.

4 Entree Servings

1 pork tenderloin (about 12 ounces), visible fat trimmed
   Honey-Mustard Dressing (recipe follows)
2 cups thinly sliced green or red cabbage
1 large apple, cored, sliced
¹/₂ cup sliced celery
¹/₄ cup thinly sliced green onions and tops
¹/₂ cup raisins
8 ounces mini-lasagne, *or* mafalde, broken into 1¹/₂-inch pieces, cooked, room temperature

1. Heat oven to 425° F. Place pork in 13 x 9-inch baking pan; brush with 2 tablespoons Honey-Mustard Dressing. Roast pork until no longer pink in center, 30 to 35 minutes. Remove pork to cutting board; let stand, loosely covered with aluminum foil, 5 minutes.

2. Combine cabbage, apple, celery, green onions, raisins, and pasta in salad bowl. Slice pork into ¹/₄-inch slices; add to pasta mixture. Pour remaining Honey-Mustard Dressing over and toss.

Honey-Mustard Dressing

Makes about ¹/₂ cup

3 tablespoons apple juice
3 tablespoons cider vinegar
2 tablespoons honey
1 tablespoon vegetable oil
2 teaspoons Dijon-style mustard
1 clove garlic, minced
¹/₈ teaspoon ground allspice
¹/₄ teaspoon salt
¹/₄ teaspoon pepper

1. Mix all ingredients; refrigerate until ready to use. Mix again before using.

Nutritional Data

PER SERVING		EXCHANGES	
Calories	330	Milk	0.0
% Calories from fat	16	Veg.	1.0
Fat (gm)	6.1	Fruit	0.0
Sat. Fat (gm)	0.9	Bread	3.0
Cholesterol (mg)	42.5	Meat	1.0
Sodium (mg)	267	Fat	0.5
Protein (gm)	1.4		
Carbohydrate (gm)	50.1		

4
SAUCES

Meal planning can become wearisome and tedious—sauce sorcery to the rescue! Select a new sauce and team it with a new pasta shape to give menus an extra spark of interest and regale flagging appetites.

RED CLAM SAUCE

———————◆———————

This light tomato sauce, rich with succulent clams, is traditionally served over linguine. If you prefer white clam sauce, see Linguine with White Clam Sauce (see pg. 88).

4 Servings (about 1/2 cup each)

2 cloves garlic, minced
1 tablespoon olive oil
1 can (28 ounces) Italian tomatoes, undrained,
    coarsely chopped
2 teaspoons dried oregano leaves
1 pound undrained, shelled baby clams, *or* 2
    cans (7½ ounces each) baby clams, undrained
¼ cup dry white wine, *or* clam juice
1 tablespoon lemon juice
⅛ to ¼ teaspoon cayenne pepper
¼ teaspoon ground black pepper

1. Saute garlic in oil in medium saucepan until tender. Stir in tomatoes with liquid and oregano; heat to boiling. Reduce heat and simmer, uncovered, until mixture is medium sauce consistency, about 10 minutes.

2. Stir in clams, wine, lemon juice, and both peppers. Simmer, covered, until clams are cooked, 5 to 7 minutes.

Nutritional Data

PER SERVING		EXCHANGES	
Calories	170	Milk	0.0
% Calories from fat	26	Veg.	2.0
(12 with 2 oz. pasta)		Fruit	0.0
Fat (gm)	5.1	Bread	0.0
Sat. Fat (gm)	0.7	Meat	2.0
Cholesterol (mg)	38.6	Fat	0.0
Sodium (mg)	388		
Protein (gm)	16.6		
Carbohydrate (gm)	13		

PEASANT BEAN SAUCE WITH TOMATOES AND SAGE

Hearty and chunky with 2 types of beans, this sauce is excellent served over one of the tube-shaped pastas such as ziti, mostaccioli, or rigatoni.

4 Servings (about 1 cup each)

1 can (15½ ounces) red kidney beans, drained
1 can (15 ounces) cannellini, *or* great northern beans, drained
½ cup chopped onions
½ cup chopped celery
2 cloves garlic, minced
1 can (16 ounces) plum tomatoes, drained, chopped
1 can (14½ ounces) low-salt chicken broth
1 teaspoon dried sage leaves
¼ teaspoon salt
⅛ teaspoon pepper

1. Heat beans, onions, celery, and garlic to boiling in large saucepan. Reduce heat and simmer, covered, 5 minutes.

2. Stir in tomatoes, chicken broth, and sage; heat to boiling. Reduce heat and simmer, uncovered, until mixture is desired sauce consistency, about 20 minutes. Stir in salt and pepper.

Nutritional Data

PER SERVING		EXCHANGES	
Calories	215	Milk	0.0
% Calories from fat	7	Veg.	1.0
(4 with 2 oz. pasta)		Fruit	0.0
Fat (gm)	2.1	Bread	2.0
Sat. Fat (gm)	0.1	Meat	1.0
Cholesterol (mg)	0	Fat	0.0
Sodium (mg)	762		
Protein (gm)	18.5		
Carbohydrate (gm)	46.8		

MARINARA SAUCE

---◆---

*A classic Italian meatless tomato sauce, seasoned
very simply. Serve over any desired pasta.*

8 Servings (about 1/2 cup each)

2 medium onions, chopped
6 to 8 cloves garlic, minced
2 tablespoons olive oil
2 cans (16 ounces each) plum tomatoes, drained,
    chopped
1/2 cup dry white wine, *or* tomato juice
1/4 cup tomato paste
2 to 3 tablespoons lemon juice
1/2 teaspoon salt
1/4 teaspoon pepper

1. Saute onions and garlic in oil in large saucepan until tender, about 5
minutes. Stir in tomatoes, wine, and tomato paste; heat to boiling.
Reduce heat and simmer, uncovered, until mixture is medium sauce
consistency, about 20 minutes. Stir in lemon juice, salt, and pepper.

Nutritional Data

PER SERVING		EXCHANGES	
Calories	85	Milk	0.0
% Calories from fat	37	Veg.	2.0
(11 with 2 oz. pasta)		Fruit	0.0
Fat (gm)	3.8	Bread	0.0
Sat. Fat (gm)	0.5	Meat	0.0
Cholesterol (mg)	0	Fat	0.5
Sodium (mg)	325		
Protein (gm)	1.9		
Carbohydrate (gm)	10.2		

TOMATO SAUCE WITH MUSHROOMS AND SHERRY

Flavors of mushrooms, sherry wine, rosemary, and oregano meld in a delicious tomato sauce. Serve over spinach fettuccine, thin spaghetti, or linguine.

4 Servings (about 1/2 cup each)

1 small onion, finely chopped
2 cloves garlic, minced
1 tablespoon olive oil
4 cups sliced mushrooms
3 tablespoons dry sherry, *or* water
1 can (28 ounces) crushed tomatoes, undrained
2 tablespoons finely chopped parsley
1/2 teaspoon dried rosemary leaves, crushed
1/2 teaspoon dried oregano leaves
1 teaspoon sugar
1/4 teaspoon salt
1/4 teaspoon pepper

1. Saute onions and garlic in oil in medium saucepan 2 to 3 minutes. Add mushrooms and sherry; cook, covered, over medium-high heat until mushrooms are wilted and release liquid. Reduce heat and cook, uncovered, until mushrooms are soft and have darkened, stirring occasionally.

2. Stir in tomatoes, herbs, and sugar; heat to boiling. Reduce heat and simmer, covered, 10 to 15 minutes. Stir in salt and pepper.

Nutritional Data

PER SERVING		EXCHANGES	
Calories	118	Milk	0.0
% Calories from fat	29	Veg.	3.0
(11 with 2 oz. pasta)		Fruit	0.0
Fat (gm)	4.2	Bread	0.0
Sat. Fat (gm)	0.6	Meat	0.0
Cholesterol (mg)	0	Fat	1.0
Sodium (mg)	462		
Protein (gm)	3.8		
Carbohydrate (gm)	16.3		

FRESH TOMATOES AND HERBS SAUCE

Prepare and enjoy this sauce when garden-ripened tomatoes are at their peak flavor. Use fresh herbs if at all possible. Serve over any desired pasta.

6 Servings *(about ¹/₂ cup each)*

¹/₄ cup finely chopped onions
3 cloves garlic, minced
1 tablespoon olive oil
5 cups peeled, seeded, chopped tomatoes
2 tablespoons finely chopped fresh basil leaves,
  or 2 teaspoons dried
1 tablespoon finely chopped fresh thyme leaves,
  or 1 teaspoon dried
1 tablespoon finely chopped fresh oregano
  leaves, *or* 1 teaspoon dried
2 bay leaves
¹/₂ teaspoon salt
¹/₂ teaspoon pepper

1. Saute onions and garlic in oil in large saucepan until tender, about 5 minutes. Add tomatoes and herbs to saucepan. Cook, covered, over medium-high heat until tomatoes release liquid and begin to wilt, about 5 minutes. Reduce heat and simmer, uncovered, until mixture is very thick, about 20 minutes. Discard bay leaves; stir in salt and pepper.

2. If a smooth sauce is desired, process in food processor or blender until smooth.

Nutritional Data

PER SERVING		EXCHANGES	
Calories	66	Milk	0.0
% Calories from fat	36	Veg.	2.0
(10 with 2 oz. pasta)		Fruit	0.0
Fat (gm)	2.9	Bread	0.0
Sat. Fat (gm)	0.4	Meat	0.0
Cholesterol (mg)	0	Fat	0.5
Sodium (mg)	106		
Protein (gm)	1.8		
Carbohydrate (gm)	10.1		

BOLOGNESE-STYLE MEAT SAUCE

Traditionally Bolognese Sauce is made with chopped or ground beef or Italian sausage. Lower-fat ground turkey is used for the "skinny" version of this sauce. A favorite with spaghetti—or use a shaped pasta such as farfalle (bow ties) or ruote (wheels).

4 Servings (about 1/2 cup each)

- 1 pound ground turkey
- 1 small onion, finely chopped
- 1/4 cup thinly sliced carrot
- 1/4 cup thinly sliced celery
- 3 cloves garlic, minced
- 1/2 teaspoon dried oregano leaves
- 1/2 teaspoon dried tarragon leaves
- 1/2 teaspoon dried thyme leaves
- 1/8 teaspoon ground nutmeg
- 1 can (8 ounces) low-sodium tomato sauce
- 1 can (8 ounces) low-sodium whole tomatoes, drained, chopped
- 1/4 cup dry white wine, *or* tomato juice
- 1/2 teaspoon salt
- 1/4 teaspoon pepper

1. Cook ground turkey in medium saucepan over medium heat until browned, 5 to 8 minutes. Remove turkey from saucepan; drain and crumble. Drain excess fat from saucepan.

2. Add next 4 vegetables to saucepan; saute until crisp-tender, about 5 minutes. Stir in herbs; cook 1 minute. Add tomato sauce, tomatoes, and wine; heat to boiling. Reduce heat and simmer, uncovered, until thick sauce consistency, about 15 minutes. Stir in salt and pepper.

Nutritional Data

PER SERVING		EXCHANGES	
Calories	202	Milk	0.0
% Calories from fat	39	Veg.	2.0
(19 with 2 oz. pasta)		Fruit	0.0
Fat (gm)	8.7	Bread	0.0
Sat. Fat (gm)	2.4	Meat	2.0
Cholesterol (mg)	42.2	Fat	1.0
Sodium (mg)	352		
Protein (gm)	17.1		
Carbohydrate (gm)	11		

Tomato and Meatball Sauce

You'll savor the full-bodied herb flavors in this updated version of a traditional meatball sauce. Serve with traditional spaghetti or one of the more unusually shaped pastas such as cappelletti ("little hats") or gnocchi.

6 Servings (about 1$^1/_3$ cups each)

1 cup chopped onions
3 cloves garlic, minced
1 tablespoon olive oil
1 can (16 ounces) low-sodium whole tomatoes, drained, chopped
1 can (8 ounces) low-sodium tomato sauce
1 tablespoon tomato paste
1 teaspoon dried basil leaves
$^1/_2$ teaspoon dried tarragon leaves
$^1/_2$ teaspoon dried oregano leaves
$^1/_8$ teaspoon crushed red pepper
$^1/_2$ teaspoon salt
$^1/_4$ teaspoon black pepper
Herb-Seasoned Meatballs (recipe follows)

1. Saute onions and garlic in oil in large saucepan 2 to 3 minutes. Stir in tomatoes, tomato sauce, tomato paste, herbs, and red pepper; heat to boiling. Reduce heat and simmer, uncovered, 10 minutes; stir in salt and pepper.

2. Add Herb-Seasoned Meatballs to tomato mixture. Simmer, uncovered, until medium sauce consistency, 10 to 15 minutes.

Herb-Seasoned Meatballs

Makes 6 servings (3 meatballs each)

1 pound ground turkey
$^1/_3$ cup unseasoned dry breadcrumbs
1 egg white
3 cloves garlic, minced
2 tablespoons minced parsley
$^3/_4$ teaspoon dried basil leaves
$^3/_4$ teaspoon dried oregano leaves

¼ teaspoon dried thyme leaves
½ teaspoon salt
¼ teaspoon pepper

1. Mix ground turkey and remaining ingredients; shape into 18 meatballs.
    Cook meatballs over medium heat in skillet until browned on all sides
    and no longer pink in the center, 8 to 10 minutes.

Nutritional Data

PER SERVING		EXCHANGES	
Calories	189	Milk	0.0
% Calories from fat	40	Veg.	2.0
(19 with 2 oz. pasta)		Fruit	0.0
Fat (gm)	8.5	Bread	0.5
Sat. Fat (gm)	1.9	Meat	1.5
Cholesterol (mg)	28.1	Fat	0.5
Sodium (mg)	484		
Protein (gm)	13.4		
Carbohydrate (gm)	14.9		

FRESH TOMATO-BASIL SAUCE

This fresh tomato sauce has an intense basil flavor. For interesting variations, other fresh herbs such as rosemary, tarragon, or sage can be substituted for the basil. Serve over a more delicate pasta, such as angel hair or thin spaghetti.

8 Servings (about 1/2 cup each)

    5 cups chopped tomatoes
    1 small onion, chopped
    5 cloves garlic, minced
  1/2 cup dry red *or* white wine
    2 tablespoons tomato paste
    1 tablespoon sugar
    2 tablespoons finely chopped fresh thyme
       leaves, *or* 1 1/2 teaspoons dried
    2 bay leaves
3 to 4 tablespoons finely chopped fresh basil leaves,
       or 2 teaspoons dried
  1/2 teaspoon salt
  1/8 teaspoon crushed red pepper
  1/4 teaspoon ground black pepper

1. Combine all ingredients, except basil, salt, and peppers, in medium saucepan; heat to boiling. Reduce heat and simmer, covered, 5 minutes. Simmer, uncovered, until sauce is reduced to medium consistency, about 20 minutes.

2. Stir in basil, salt, and both peppers; simmer 5 to 10 minutes longer. Discard bay leaves.

Nutritional Data

PER SERVING		EXCHANGES	
Calories	58	Milk	0.0
% Calories from fat	8	Veg.	2.0
(2 with 2 oz. pasta)		Fruit	0.0
Fat (gm)	0.6	Bread	0.0
Sat. Fat (gm)	0.1	Meat	0.0
Cholesterol (mg)	0	Fat	0.0
Sodium (mg)	122		
Protein (gm)	1.7		
Carbohydrate (gm)	10.9		

CIOPPINO SAUCE

Feel free to substitute other kinds of fresh fish, according to season, availability, and price. The seafood is added to the sauce toward the end of the cooking time to avoid overcooking.

6 Servings (about 1 cup each)

1 cup chopped green bell peppers
1 cup chopped onions
1 cup sliced mushrooms
4 cloves garlic, minced
1 tablespoon olive oil
3 cups chopped tomatoes
1/2 cup dry white wine, *or* clam juice
1 tablespoon tomato paste
2 tablespoons finely chopped parsley
2 teaspoons dried oregano leaves
2 teaspoons dried basil leaves
1 teaspoon ground turmeric
8 ounces sea scallops
8 ounces crab meat, flaked into 1/2-inch pieces
1 halibut, *or* haddock steak (4 ounces), cut into 1-inch pieces
12 mussels in the shell, scrubbed
1/2 teaspoon salt
1/4 teaspoon pepper

1. Saute bell pepper, onions, mushrooms, and garlic in oil in large saucepan until onions are tender, about 5 minutes. Stir in tomatoes, wine, tomato paste, and herbs; heat to boiling. Reduce heat and simmer, covered, 5 minutes. Simmer, uncovered, 20 minutes more, until mixture is thickened to desired consistency.

2. Add seafood last 10 to 15 minutes of cooking time. Stir in salt and pepper. Spoon sauce over pasta served in bowls.

Nutritional Data

PER SERVING		EXCHANGES	
Calories	196	Milk	0.0
% Calories from fat	21	Veg.	3.0
(10 with 2 oz. pasta)		Fruit	0.0
Fat (gm)	4.7	Bread	0.0
Sat. Fat (gm)	0.6	Meat	2.0
Cholesterol (mg)	39.5	Fat	0.0
Sodium (mg)	386		
Protein (gm)	20.8		
Carbohydrate (gm)	15.6		

PEPPERONATA-TOMATO SAUCE

Italian peperonata, a slow-cooked mixture of bell peppers and onions, is combined with tomato sauce for a perfect pasta topping.

4 Servings (about ¹/₂ cup each)

1 medium red bell pepper, sliced
1 medium green bell pepper, sliced
1 medium yellow bell pepper, sliced
1 medium onion, sliced
3 cloves garlic, minced
2 tablespoons olive oil
2 tablespoons water
2 cans (8 ounces each) low-sodium
   tomato sauce
¹/₂ teaspoon salt
¹/₄ teaspoon pepper

1. Saute bell peppers, onions, and garlic in oil in medium saucepan 2 to 3 minutes. Add water; cook, covered, over medium to medium-high heat until peppers are wilted. Cook, uncovered, over medium-low heat until peppers mixture and onions are very soft and browned, about 20 minutes.

2. Stir tomato sauce into peppers mixture; heat to boiling. Reduce heat and simmer, uncovered, until mixture is thick sauce consistency, 10 to 15 minutes. Stir in salt and pepper.

Nutritional Data

PER SERVING		EXCHANGES	
Calories	135	Milk	0.0
% Calories from fat	45	Veg.	3.0
(18 with 2 oz. pasta)		Fruit	0.0
Fat (gm)	6.9	Bread	0.0
Sat. Fat (gm)	0.9	Meat	0.0
Cholesterol (mg)	0	Fat	1.5
Sodium (mg)	302		
Protein (gm)	3		
Carbohydrate (gm)	16		

CREOLE SAUCE

Creole flavors accent this substantial sauce. If you enjoy okra, it would be an excellent addition. Serve over spaghetti or tube-shaped pasta.

8 Servings (about 1/2 cup each)

1½ cups sliced green bell pepper
¾ cup sliced carrots
½ cup sliced onions
½ cup sliced celery
3 cloves garlic, minced
2 tablespoons olive oil
1 medium tomato, chopped
1 teaspoon dried basil leaves
1 teaspoon dried oregano leaves
1 teaspoon paprika
½ teaspoon dried thyme leaves
½ teaspoon gumbo file powder (optional)
1 bay leaf
¼ teaspoon cayenne pepper
½ teaspoon salt
1 can (14½ ounces) low-sodium chicken broth
1 can (8 ounces) low-sodium tomato sauce

1. Saute bell pepper, carrots, onions, celery, and garlic in oil until peppers are tender, 8 to 10 minutes. Stir in tomato, combined herbs, gumbo file powder, bay leaf, cayenne pepper, and salt. Cook over medium heat 2 to 3 minutes, stirring frequently.

2. Add chicken broth and tomato sauce; heat to boiling. Reduce heat and simmer, uncovered, until vegetables are tender and sauce is thickened to desired consistency, about 20 minutes. Discard bay leaf.

Nutritional Data

PER SERVING		EXCHANGES	
Calories	72	Milk	0.0
% Calories from fat	44	Veg.	2.0
(12 with 2 oz. pasta)		Fruit	0.0
Fat (gm)	3.7	Bread	0.0
Sat. Fat (gm)	0.5	Meat	0.0
Cholesterol (mg)	0	Fat	0.5
Sodium (mg)	162		
Protein (gm)	1.7		
Carbohydrate (gm)	8.9		

EGGPLANT SAUCE

♦

Tarragon and thyme replace the customary basil in this popular tomato-based eggplant sauce. The eggplant can be peeled or not, as you prefer.

12 Servings (about ¹/₂ cup each)

1 pound unpeeled eggplant, cut into 1¹/₂-inch pieces
1 cup chopped onions
¹/₂ cup chopped green bell pepper
6 cloves garlic, minced
2 tablespoons olive oil
3 cups chopped tomatoes
³/₄ teaspoon dried tarragon leaves
³/₄ teaspoon dried thyme leaves
1 can (28 ounces) crushed tomatoes, undrained
¹/₂ cup dry red wine
2 tablespoons drained capers
2 teaspoons sugar
¹/₂ teaspoon salt
¹/₄ teaspoon pepper

1. Saute eggplant, onions, bell pepper, and garlic in oil in large saucepan 5 minutes. Add chopped tomatoes and herbs, and saute until onions are crisp-tender, 5 to 7 minutes.

2. Stir canned tomatoes, wine, capers, and sugar into vegetable mixture; heat to boiling. Reduce heat and simmer, covered, until eggplant is tender, about 20 minutes. Simmer, uncovered, until desired sauce consistency, about 10 minutes more. Stir in salt and pepper.

Nutritional Data

PER SERVING		EXCHANGES	
Calories	80	Milk	0.0
% Calories from fat	28	Veg.	2.0
(8 with 2 oz. pasta)		Fruit	0.0
Fat (gm)	2.7	Bread	0.0
Sat. Fat (gm)	0.3	Meat	0.0
Cholesterol (mg)	0	Fat	0.5
Sodium (mg)	255		
Protein (gm)	1.9		
Carbohydrate (gm)	12		

CINCINNATI CHILI SAUCE

5-Way Cincinnati Chili gained fame in the chili parlors of St. Louis. The sauce is seasoned with sweet spices and generally has a hint of dark chocolate. The chili is served alone, 1 way; 2 ways, over spaghetti; 3 ways, with added beans; 4 ways, with chopped onions; 5 ways, with shredded cheese!

8 Servings (about 1/2 cup each)

12 ounces ground turkey
1/2 cup chopped onions
4 cloves garlic, minced
1 can (28 ounces) crushed tomatoes, undrained
1 can (8 ounces) low-sodium tomato sauce
1/2 cup water
2 tablespoons chili powder
2 teaspoons dried oregano leaves
1 teaspoon ground cinnamon
1 teaspoon ground allspice
1/2 teaspoon paprika
1 tablespoon cocoa
1/2 teaspoon salt
1/2 teaspoon pepper

1. Cook turkey in large saucepan over medium heat until browned, 5 to 8 minutes. Remove turkey from saucepan; drain and crumble. Drain excess fat from saucepan.

2. Add onions and garlic to saucepan; saute until onions are tender, about 5 minutes. Stir in turkey and remaining ingredients; heat to boiling. Reduce heat and simmer, covered, 15 minutes; simmer, uncovered, until sauce is thickened, about 15 minutes more.

Nutritional Data

PER SERVING		EXCHANGES	
Calories	111	Milk	0.0
% Calories from fat	30	Veg.	2.5
(11 with 2 oz. pasta)		Fruit	0.0
Fat (gm)	3.9	Bread	0.0
Sat. Fat (gm)	0.9	Meat	0.5
Cholesterol (mg)	15.8	Fat	0.5
Sodium (mg)	411		
Protein (gm)	8		
Carbohydrate (gm)	12.1		

PAPRIKASH SAUCE

Suit your preference of hot or sweet paprika in this recipe. Reduced-fat sour cream adds a wonderful creamy texture and richness to the sauce. Serve over any kind of pasta.

6 Servings (about ½ cup each)

1 medium red bell pepper, sliced
1 medium green bell pepper, sliced
1 large onion, sliced
1 tablespoon margarine
2 tablespoons flour
1 tablespoon sweet Hungarian paprika
½ teaspoon salt
¼ teaspoon pepper
1 can (8 ounces) low-sodium tomato sauce
½ cup canned low-salt chicken broth
½ cup dry white wine, *or* canned low-salt chicken broth
½ cup reduced-fat sour cream

1. Cook bell pepper and onions in margarine in large skillet over medium heat until peppers are very soft, 10 to 15 minutes. Stir in flour, paprika, salt, and pepper; cook 3 to 5 minutes, stirring occasionally.

2. Stir in tomato sauce, chicken broth, and wine; heat to boiling. Reduce heat and simmer, uncovered, until sauce is thickened, 5 to 7 minutes. Stir in sour cream.

Nutritional Data

PER SERVING		EXCHANGES	
Calories	98	Milk	0.0
% Calories from fat	32	Veg.	2.0
(10 with 2 oz. pasta)		Fruit	0.0
Fat (gm)	3.4	Bread	0.0
Sat. Fat (gm)	0.4	Meat	0.0
Cholesterol (mg)	6.3	Fat	1.0
Sodium (mg)	229		
Protein (gm)	2.4		
Carbohydrate (gm)	11		

ALFREDO SAUCE

◆

Serve this famous Parmesan-flavored sauce
over traditional fettuccine noodles.

4 Servings (about ¹/₂ cup each)

  3 tablespoons margarine
 ¹/₄ cup all-purpose flour
2¹/₂ cups skim milk
 ¹/₄ cup grated Parmesan cheese
 ¹/₈ teaspoon ground nutmeg
 ¹/₂ teaspoon salt
 ¹/₄ teaspoon pepper

1. Melt margarine in medium saucepan; stir in flour. Cook over medium heat 1 minute, stirring constantly. Stir in milk; heat to boiling. Boil, stirring constantly, until thickened, 1 to 2 minutes.

2. Reduce heat to low and stir in cheese, nutmeg, salt, and pepper; cook 1 to 2 minutes.

Nutritional Data

PER SERVING		EXCHANGES	
Calories	187	Milk	0.5
% Calories from fat	52	Veg.	0.0
(24 with 2 oz. pasta)		Fruit	0.0
Fat (gm)	10.7	Bread	0.5
Sat. Fat (gm)	3.1	Meat	0.5
Cholesterol (mg)	7.4	Fat	2.0
Sodium (mg)	561		
Protein (gm)	8.7		
Carbohydrate (gm)	13.9		

GORGONZOLA SAUCE

+

*Although higher in fat content than some of the other blue cheeses,
Gorgonzola lends richness of flavor to this "creamy" sauce.*

6 Servings (about 1/3 cup each)

3 tablespoons margarine
1/4 cup all-purpose flour
2 cups skim milk
1/4 cup dry white wine, *or* skim milk
3 ounces Gorgonzola cheese, crumbled
1/4 teaspoon pepper

1. Melt margarine in medium saucepan; stir in flour. Cook over medium heat 1 minute, stirring constantly. Stir in milk and wine; heat to boiling. Boil, stirring constantly, until thickened, 1 to 2 minutes.

2. Reduce heat to low, and stir in cheese and pepper; cook 1 to 2 minutes.

Nutritional Data

PER SERVING		EXCHANGES	
Calories	156	Milk	0.0
% Calories from fat	59	Veg.	0.0
(24 with 2 oz. pasta)		Fruit	0.0
Fat (gm)	10.2	Bread	0.5
Sat. Fat (gm)	1.2	Meat	0.5
Cholesterol (mg)	14	Fat	2.0
Sodium (mg)	271		
Protein (gm)	6.4		
Carbohydrate (gm)	8.1		

CREAMED SPINACH SAUCE

A versatile sauce, it can be used to embellish sauteed vegetables, cubed chicken, or seafood. The sauce clings nicely, so serve over a substantial pasta such as farfalle (bow ties), radiatore, or a filled tortelloni.

6 Servings (about 1/2 cup each)

2	cloves garlic, minced
2	tablespoons margarine
1/4	cup all-purpose flour
3	cups 2% milk
1 1/2	pounds fresh spinach, cleaned, chopped
2	teaspoons dried basil leaves
1/8 to 1/4	teaspoon ground nutmeg
4 to 6	dashes red pepper sauce
1/4 to 1/2	teaspoon salt

1. Saute garlic in margarine in large saucepan 1 to 2 minutes. Stir in flour and cook over medium heat 1 to 2 minutes more. Stir in milk; heat to boiling. Boil, stirring constantly, until thickened, 1 to 2 minutes.

2. Stir spinach and remaining ingredients into sauce. Cook, uncovered, over medium heat until spinach is cooked, 5 to 7 minutes.

Nutritional Data

PER SERVING		EXCHANGES	
Calories	141	Milk	0.5
% Calories from fat	40	Veg.	2.0
(17 with 2 oz. pasta)		Fruit	0.0
Fat (gm)	6.6	Bread	0.0
Sat. Fat (gm)	2.8	Meat	0.0
Cholesterol (mg)	9	Fat	1.0
Sodium (mg)	284		
Protein (gm)	8		
Carbohydrate (gm)	14.4		

PRIMAVERA SAUCE

Select vegetables from the season's bounty for this rich,
flavorful sauce. Serve over fettuccine, linguine, or spaghetti.

4 Servings (about 1¹/₂ cups each)

3 tablespoons margarine
¹/₄ cup all-purpose flour
2 cups 2% milk
¹/₄ cup dry white wine, *or* low-salt chicken broth
2 cups broccoli florets, steamed until
    crisp-tender
2 cups cauliflower florets, steamed until
    crisp-tender
1 cup diagonally sliced carrots, steamed until
    crisp-tender
1 medium red bell pepper, sliced
¹/₄ cup grated Parmesan cheese
¹/₄ to ¹/₂ teaspoon ground nutmeg
¹/₄ teaspoon salt
¹/₄ teaspoon pepper

1. Melt margarine in medium saucepan; stir in flour. Cook over medium heat 1 minute, stirring constantly. Stir in milk and wine; heat to boiling. Boil, stirring constantly, until thickened, 1 to 2 minutes.

2. Stir in vegetables; cook over medium heat until hot through, 2 to 3 minutes. Reduce heat to low and stir in cheese, nutmeg, salt, and pepper; cook 1 to 2 minutes more.

Nutritional Data

PER SERVING		EXCHANGES	
Calories	256	Milk	0.5
% Calories from fat	45	Veg.	2.0
(26 with 2 oz. pasta)		Fruit	0.0
Fat (gm)	13.2	Bread	0.5
Sat. Fat (gm)	4.4	Meat	0.5
Cholesterol (mg)	14	Fat	2.0
Sodium (mg)	456		
Protein (gm)	11.3		
Carbohydrate (gm)	23		

THREE-ONION SAUCE

---◆---

*This onion mixture is cooked very slowly until
the onions are caramelized and golden.*

4 Servings (about 1/2 cup each)

1½ cups cleaned, sliced leeks
1½ cups chopped red onions
  6 shallots, sliced
  3 tablespoons olive oil
 ¼ cup all-purpose flour
  1 can (14½ ounces) low-salt chicken broth
 ¼ teaspoon dried thyme leaves
 ½ teaspoon salt
 ¼ teaspoon pepper

1. Saute leeks, onions, and shallots in oil in medium saucepan 2 to 3 minutes. Reduce heat to medium-low and cook slowly until mixture is golden brown. Stir in flour; cook over medium heat 1 to 2 minutes more.

2. Stir chicken broth, thyme, salt and pepper into leek mixture; heat to boiling. Boil, stirring constantly, until thickened, 1 to 2 minutes.

Nutritional Data

PER SERVING		EXCHANGES	
Calories	185	Milk	0.0
% Calories from fat	50	Veg.	2.0
(24 with 2 oz. pasta)		Fruit	0.0
Fat (gm)	10.7	Bread	0.5
Sat. Fat (gm)	1.4	Meat	0.0
Cholesterol (mg)	0	Fat	2.0
Sodium (mg)	294		
Protein (gm)	3.1		
Carbohydrate (gm)	21		

MANY-CLOVES GARLIC SAUCE

Cooked slowly until caramelized, the garlic becomes very sweet in flavor.

4 Servings (about 1/2 cup each)

- 25 cloves garlic, peeled
- 2 tablespoons olive oil
- 2 tablespoons flour
- 1 can (15 ounces) low-salt chicken broth
- 1/4 cup dry white wine, *or* low-salt chicken broth
- 2 tablespoons finely chopped parsley
- 1/8 teaspoon salt
- 2 dashes ground white pepper

1. Saute garlic in oil in medium skillet 2 to 3 minutes. Reduce heat to medium-low, and cook slowly until garlic cloves are golden brown. Mash cloves slightly with fork.

2. Stir flour into garlic mixture; cook over medium heat 1 to 2 minutes. Stir in chicken broth and wine; heat to boiling. Boil, stirring constantly, until thickened, 1 to 2 minutes. Stir in parsley, salt, and pepper.

Nutritional Data

PER SERVING		EXCHANGES	
Calories	118	Milk	0.0
% Calories from fat	53	Veg.	2.0
(19 with 2 oz. pasta)		Fruit	0.0
Fat (gm)	7.1	Bread	0.0
Sat. Fat (gm)	0.9	Meat	0.0
Cholesterol (mg)	0	Fat	1.5
Sodium (mg)	87		
Protein (gm)	2.2		
Carbohydrate (gm)	9.8		

ARTICHOKE SAUCE

---

*Minced jalapeño peppers adds a hint of
piquancy to this sauce. Serve over fusilli (spirals),
rotini (corkscrews), or other-shaped pastas.*

4 Servings (about ¹/₂ cup each)

1 cup sliced onions
2 cloves garlic, minced
1 tablespoon olive oil
1 can (14 ounces) artichoke hearts, drained,
   rinsed, and sliced
¹/₄ teaspoon minced, seeded jalapeño peppers
2 tablespoons flour
1 cup canned low-salt chicken broth
¹/₄ cup grated Parmesan cheese
2 tablespoons finely chopped parsley
¹/₄ teaspoon salt
¹/₄ teaspoon pepper

1. Saute onions and garlic in oil in medium saucepan until tender, about
5 minutes. Stir in artichoke hearts and jalapeño peppers; cook over
medium heat 10 minutes. Stir in flour; cook 1 to 2 minutes more.

2. Stir chicken broth into artichoke mixture; heat to boiling. Boil, stirring
constantly, until thickened, 1 to 2 minutes.

3. Reduce heat to low, and stir in Parmesan cheese, parsley, salt, and
pepper; cook 1 to 2 minutes.

Nutritional Data

PER SERVING		EXCHANGES	
Calories	143	Milk	0.0
% Calories from fat	33	Veg.	3.0
(15 with 2 oz. pasta)		Fruit	0.0
Fat (gm)	5.8	Bread	0.0
Sat. Fat (gm)	1.7	Meat	0.5
Cholesterol (mg)	4.9	Fat	1.0
Sodium (mg)	357		
Protein (gm)	7.4		
Carbohydrate (gm)	18.7		

WILD MUSHROOM SAUCE

If porcini mushrooms are not available, shiitaki or portobello mushrooms may be substituted. The wide pappardelle noodles or fettuccine are excellent choices with this full-flavored sauce.

4 Servings (about 1/2 cup each)

2 cups sliced cremini *or* white mushrooms
1 cup sliced porcini *or* shiitaki mushrooms
6 shallots, *or* green onions, finely chopped
2 teaspoons dried basil leaves
3/4 teaspoon dried thyme leaves
1 can (14 1/2 ounces) low-salt chicken broth, divided
2 tablespoons dry white wine (optional)
1 tablespoon minced parsley
2 to 3 dashes red pepper sauce
1/4 teaspoon salt

1. Combine mushrooms, shallots, herbs, and 3 tablespoons chicken broth in large skillet. Cook, covered, over medium-high heat until mushrooms are wilted and release liquid. Cook, uncovered, until mushrooms are soft and have darkened, stirring occasionally.

2. Add remaining chicken broth and wine to skillet; heat to boiling. Reduce heat and simmer, uncovered, until liquid is reduced by about one-third, 10 to 12 minutes. Stir in parsley, red pepper sauce, and salt.

Nutritional Data

PER SERVING		EXCHANGES	
Calories	48	Milk	0.0
% Calories from fat	8	Veg.	2.0
(2 with 2 oz. pasta)		Fruit	0.0
Fat (gm)	0.5	Bread	0.0
Sat. Fat (gm)	0.1	Meat	0.0
Cholesterol (mg)	0	Fat	0.0
Sodium (mg)	154		
Protein (gm)	2.3		
Carbohydrate (gm)	10.3		

ROASTED RED PEPPER SAUCE

Jarred roasted red bell peppers can be substituted for the fresh; drain well and puree according to recipe directions.

4 Servings (about 1/2 cup each)

4 medium red bell peppers
1 clove garlic, minced
1 cup canned low-salt chicken broth
1/4 teaspoon salt
1/4 teaspoon ground white pepper

1. Heat oven to 425° F. Cut bell peppers into halves; remove and discard seeds and veins. Place peppers, cut sides down, in 13 x 9-inch baking pan. Bake peppers until blackened and skins are blistered, about 15 minutes. Place peppers in plastic bag and let stand 5 to 10 minutes; peel off skin and discard.

2. Process peppers and garlic in food processor or blender until smooth. Transfer pepper mixture to saucepan. Stir in chicken broth and heat to boiling. Reduce heat and simmer, uncovered, until mixture is medium sauce consistency, about 10 minutes. Stir in salt and pepper.

Nutritional Data

PER SERVING		EXCHANGES	
Calories	24	Milk	0.0
% Calories from fat	8	Veg.	1.0
(1 with 2 oz. pasta)		Fruit	0.0
Fat (gm)	0.2	Bread	0.0
Sat. Fat (gm)	0	Meat	0.0
Cholesterol (mg)	0	Fat	0.0
Sodium (mg)	143		
Protein (gm)	1.1		
Carbohydrate (gm)	5.3		

MIXED HERB PESTO

Packaged fresh herbs are readily available in most supermarkets. Each 1/2-ounce package yields about 1/4 cup of packed herb leaves. Serve pesto sauces at room temperature, mixing with hot pasta.

4 Servings (about 2 tablespoons each)

1/2 cup packed fresh basil leaves, *or* 2 tablespoons dried
1/2 cup packed fresh parsley leaves
1/4 cup packed fresh oregano leaves, *or* 2 tablespoons dried
3 cloves garlic, minced
2 tablespoons grated Parmesan cheese
1 ounce walnuts (about 14 medium)
2 tablespoons olive oil
2 teaspoons lemon juice
1/2 teaspoon salt
1/4 teaspoon pepper

1. Combine herbs, garlic, Parmesan cheese, and walnuts in food processor or blender. Process, adding oil and lemon gradually, until mixture is very finely chopped. Stir in salt and pepper.

Nutritional Data

PER SERVING		EXCHANGES	
Calories	134	Milk	0.0
% Calories from fat	77	Veg.	1.0
(31 with 2 oz. pasta)		Fruit	0.0
Fat (gm)	12	Bread	0.0
Sat. Fat (gm)	1.9	Meat	0.0
Cholesterol (mg)	2.4	Fat	2.5
Sodium (mg)	330		
Protein (gm)	4		
Carbohydrate (gm)	4.9		

CILANTRO PESTO

◆

*A pesto with a very "fresh" flavor. As with any pesto, serve at
room temperature, adding it to hot pasta. The flavor of
dried cilantro is not acceptable in this recipe; if the fresh
herb is not available, substitute fresh tarragon or oregano.*

6 Servings (about 2 tablespoons each)

1½ cups packed cilantro leaves
½ cup packed parsley
1 clove garlic, minced
¼ cup grated Parmesan cheese
3 tablespoons pine nuts, *or* walnuts
1 tablespoon olive oil
1 tablespoon lemon juice
¼ teaspoon salt
¼ teaspoon pepper

1. Combine herbs, garlic, Parmesan cheese, and pine nuts in food processor or blender. Process, adding oil and lemon juice gradually, until mixture is very finely chopped. Stir in salt and pepper.

Nutritional Data

PER SERVING		EXCHANGES	
Calories	70	Milk	0.0
% Calories from fat	73	Veg.	0.5
(20 with 2 oz. pasta)		Fruit	0.0
Fat (gm)	6.1	Bread	0.0
Sat. Fat (gm)	1.1	Meat	0.0
Cholesterol (mg)	3.3	Fat	1.5
Sodium (mg)	173		
Protein (gm)	3.5		
Carbohydrate (gm)	1.7		

SUN-DRIED TOMATO PESTO

Use yellow or red sun-dried tomatoes in this flavorful pesto.

4 Servings

$\frac{1}{2}$ cup sun-dried tomatoes (not in oil)
$\frac{1}{2}$ cup boiling water
$\frac{1}{2}$ cup packed basil leaves
 2 cloves garlic
 3 tablespoons olive oil
 2 tablespoons grated fat-free Parmesan cheese

1. Soak tomatoes in boiling water in bowl until softened, about 10 minutes. Drain, reserving liquid.

2. Process tomatoes, basil, garlic, oil, and cheese in food processor or blender, adding enough reserved liquid to make a smooth, spoonable paste.

Nutritional Data

PER SERVING		EXCHANGES	
Calories	118	Milk	0.0
% Calories from fat	75	Veg.	0.0
(28 with 2 oz. pasta)		Fruit	0.0
Fat (gm)	10.4	Bread	0.5
Sat. fat (gm)	1.4	Meat	0.0
Cholesterol (mg)	0	Fat	2.0
Sodium (mg)	164		
Protein (gm)	2.2		
Carbohydrate (gm)	5.5		

MINTED PESTO

Try this pesto using different mints, such as peppermint, spearmint, lemon mint, etc. The refreshing flavor is a complement to vegetables and salads as well as pasta dishes.

8 Servings (about 2 tablespoons each)

1	cup packed mint leaves
1/2	cup fresh parsley
2	cloves garlic, minced
2	tablespoons grated fat-free Parmesan cheese
2	tablespoons walnut pieces
2 to 4	tablespoons olive oil
	White pepper, to taste
2 to 3	tablespoons low-salt chicken broth, *or* water

1. Process all ingredients, except pepper and broth, in food processor or blender until smooth; season to taste with pepper.

2. Stir in enough chicken broth to make spoonable consistency.

Nutritional Data

PER SERVING		EXCHANGES	
Calories	52	Milk	0.0
% Calories from fat	78	Veg	0.0
(19 with 2 oz. pasta)		Fruit	0.0
Fat (gm)	4.6	Bread	0.0
Sat. fat (gm)	0.5	Meat	0.0
Cholesterol (mg)	0	Fat	1.0
Sodium (mg)	20		
Protein (gm)	1.3		
Carbohydrate (gm)	1.7		

5
ENTRÉES

The Italian term *al dente* means firm to the bite, or tooth, which is the precise doneness pasta should be. Fresh pastas, now readily available refrigerated or dried in most supermarkets and Italian specialty shops, cook *much* more quickly than packaged brands of dried pasta. Refrigerated fresh pasta requires only 1 to 3 minutes cooking time once cooking water returns to boiling; dried fresh pasta requires only a minute or so longer.

Packaged brands of dried pasta can require 7 to 12 minutes of cooking, depending upon the pasta type and shape. To be certain pasta is not overcooked, a good general rule is to start checking doneness halfway through the cooking time indicated in the directions.

LINGUINE WITH WHITE CLAM SAUCE

One of Italy's most treasured dishes!

4 Servings

     3 cloves garlic, minced
     1 tablespoon olive oil
     2 tablespoons cornstarch
     2 cups clam juice
    ¼ cup dry white wine
     1 pound drained clams, *or* 2 cans (7 ½ ounces
         each) baby clams, undrained
     1 tablespoon lemon juice
     1 tablespoon finely chopped parsley
1 to 2 teaspoons dried basil leaves
    ⅛ teaspoon ground white pepper
     8 ounces linguine, cooked, warm

1. Saute garlic in oil in medium saucepan, 1 to 2 minutes. Mix cornstarch and clam juice; stir into saucepan. Stir in wine and heat to boiling; boil, stirring constantly, until thickened, about 1 minute.

2. Add clams and remaining ingredients, except linguine, to juice mixture. Simmer, covered, until clams are cooked, 5 to 7 minutes. Serve over linguine.

Nutritional Data

PER SERVING		EXCHANGES	
Calories	319	Milk	0.0
% Calories from fat	18	Veg.	0.5
Fat (gm)	6.5	Fruit	0.0
Sat. Fat (gm)	0.6	Bread	2.5
Cholesterol (mg)	38.6	Meat	2.0
Sodium (mg)	305	Fat	0.5
Protein (gm)	23.5		
Carbohydrate (gm)	39.1		

JERK CHICKEN AND SHRIMP WITH LINGUINE

Enjoy the highly seasoned flavors of the Caribbean in this pasta dish!

4 Servings

8 ounces chicken tenders (skinless white meat)
4 ounces peeled, deveined shrimp
Jerk Sauce (recipe follows)
1 can (14½ ounces) low-salt chicken broth
2 teaspoons lime juice
1 pound broccoli florets, steamed until crisp-tender
8 ounces linguine, cooked, warm

1. Place chicken and shrimp in shallow glass baking dish. Spoon Jerk Sauce over and toss to coat chicken and shrimp. Refrigerate, covered, 30 minutes.

2. Transfer undrained chicken and shrimp to large skillet. Cook over medium-high heat until chicken and shrimp are cooked, about 5 minutes. Stir remaining ingredients, except linguine, into skillet; heat to boiling. Reduce heat and simmer, uncovered, until liquid is thin sauce consistency, 5 to 7 minutes.

3. Spoon chicken, shrimp, and sauce over linguine on rimmed serving platter.

Jerk Sauce

Makes about ⅓ cup

3 tablespoons water
2 tablespoons finely chopped cilantro leaves
2 tablespoons minced ginger root
2 cloves garlic, minced
2 tablespoons packed brown sugar
1 tablespoon ground allspice
2 teaspoons black peppercorns
¼ to ½ teaspoon crushed red pepper
¼ teaspoon ground coriander
¼ teaspoon ground mace

1. Process all ingredients in food processor or blender until coarse paste is formed. Refrigerate until ready to use.

Nutritional Data

PER SERVING		EXCHANGES	
Calories	332	Milk	0.0
% Calories from fat	13	Veg.	2.0
Fat (gm)	4.9	Fruit	0.0
Sat. Fat (gm)	0.6	Bread	2.5
Cholesterol (mg)	73	Meat	2.0
Sodium (mg)	232	Fat	0.0
Protein (gm)	28		
Carbohydrate (gm)	47		

SHRIMP AND PASTA SKILLET CAKES

*Crab meat or cooked, shredded chicken breast can
be substituted for the shrimp, cooked orzo for the pasta.*

4 Servings

     8 ounces finely chopped, peeled, deveined,
       cooked shrimp
     1 cup cooked linguine, *or* spaghetti, cut into
       1/2-inch pieces
   3/4 cup no-cholesterol real egg product
   1/2 cup dry plain breadcrumbs
   1/4 cup finely chopped onions
   1/2 cup finely chopped red bell pepper
     2 tablespoons finely chopped parsley
   1/2 teaspoon dried tarragon, *or* cilantro
     1 small jalapeño chili, finely chopped
   1/2 teaspoon salt (optional)
   1/4 teaspoon white pepper
   1/8 teaspoon cayenne pepper
       Vegetable cooking spray
       Lemon Herb Mayonnaise (recipe follows)

1. Mix all ingredients, except cooking spray and Lemon Herb Mayonnaise, in bowl.

2. Spray 7- or 8-inch skillet with cooking spray; heat over medium heat

until hot. Spoon half the mixture into skillet, pressing into an even layer with a pancake turner. Cook over medium heat until browned on the bottom, 3 to 4 minutes. Invert cake onto plate; slide cake back into skillet and cook until browned on the bottom, 3 to 4 minutes. Repeat with remaining mixture.

3. Cut cakes into halves; serve with Lemon Herb Mayonnaise.

Lemon Herb Mayonnaise

About ³/₄ cup

½ cup fat-free mayonnaise
¼ cup fat-free sour cream
1 to 2 teaspoons lemon juice
1 teaspoon grated lemon rind
½ teaspoon dried tarragon leaves
⅛ teaspoon dried thyme leaves

1. Mix all ingredients; refrigerate until serving time.

Nutritional Data

PER SERVING		EXCHANGES	
Calories	221	Milk	0.0
% Calories from fat	8	Veg.	1.0
Fat (gm)	2	Fruit	0.0
Sat. fat (gm)	0.3	Bread	1.5
Cholesterol (mg)	111	Meat	2.0
Sodium (mg)	751	Fat	0.0
Protein (gm)	21		
Carbohydrate (gm)	29.5		

BEEF BOURGUIGNONNE WITH PASTA

Beef, oven-simmered to tenderness in a Burgundy wine sauce, is served over mafalde, or wide egg noodles.

6 Servings

1½ pounds beef eye of round *or* tip roast, visible fat trimmed, cut into 1½-inch cubes
¼ cup all-purpose flour
1 tablespoon olive oil, *or* vegetable oil
1 cup Burgundy wine, *or* low-salt beef broth
1 cup water
1½ cups peeled pearl onions
3 cups julienne carrots
8 ounces medium mushrooms
1 teaspoon dried marjoram leaves
1 teaspoon dried thyme leaves
2 bay leaves
½ teaspoon salt
¼ teaspoon pepper
16 ounces mafalde, *or* wide egg noodles, cooked, warm

1. Coat beef cubes with flour. Saute in oil in Dutch oven until browned on all sides, about 10 minutes. Add wine and water; heat to boiling.

2. Heat oven to 325° F. Transfer Dutch oven to oven and bake, covered, until beef is tender, about 2 hours. Add vegetables, herbs, salt, and pepper during last 30 minutes of cooking time. Discard bay leaves.

3. Serve beef mixture over noodles.

Nutritional Data

PER SERVING		EXCHANGES	
Calories	507	Milk	0.0
% Calories from fat	16	Veg.	2.0
Fat (gm)	8.8	Fruit	0.0
Sat. Fat (gm)	2.1	Bread	4.0
Cholesterol (mg)	120.2	Meat	3.0
Sodium (mg)	288	Fat	0.0
Protein (gm)	34.9		
Carbohydrate (gm)	65		

PASTA WITH CABBAGE AND POTATOES

A nourishing meatless entree. For those who prefer heartier fare,
12 ounces of cubed baked ham (not included in the Nutritional
Data) can be sauteed in olive oil cooking spray and added.

6 Servings

- 6 cups thinly sliced cabbage
- 4 cloves garlic, minced
- 1/3 cup dry white wine, *or* canned low-salt chicken broth
- 4 medium Idaho potatoes, peeled, cooked, cut into 1/2-inch cubes
- 1 teaspoon dried rosemary leaves
- 1 teaspoon dried sage leaves
- 1/2 teaspoon salt
- 1/4 teaspoon pepper
- 12 ounces pappardelle, *or* other wide pasta, cooked, warm
- 1/4 cup grated Parmesan cheese
- 1 tablespoon finely chopped parsley

1. Combine cabbage, garlic, and wine in large skillet; heat to boiling. Cook, covered, over medium-high heat until cabbage is wilted, about 5 minutes; cook, uncovered, 5 minutes more.

2. Stir potatoes, herbs, salt, and pepper into cabbage mixture. Cook over medium to medium-high heat until excess liquid is gone, about 10 minutes.

3. Spoon mixture over pasta and toss; sprinkle with Parmesan cheese and toss. Sprinkle with parsley.

Nutritional Data

PER SERVING		EXCHANGES	
Calories	321	Milk	0.0
% Calories from fat	9	Veg.	2.0
Fat (gm)	3.1	Fruit	0.0
Sat. Fat (gm)	1.1	Bread	3.5
Cholesterol (mg)	3.3	Meat	0.0
Sodium (mg)	283	Fat	0.5
Protein (gm)	12		
Carbohydrate (gm)	60		

CHICKEN CACCIATORE

---

*Often served over flat pasta, Cacciatore is substantial
enough to serve over any of the shaped pastas, too.*

6 Servings

1½ pounds chicken drumsticks and thighs, skin
   removed
¼ cup all-purpose flour
   Olive oil cooking spray
   Fresh Tomatoes and Herbs Sauce
   (see pg. 62)
1 cup chopped onions
1 teaspoon ground cinnamon
12 ounces linguine, cooked, warm

1. Coat chicken pieces with flour. Spray large Dutch oven with cooking
   spray; heat over medium heat until hot. Cook chicken over medium
   heat until browned on all sides, about 15 minutes.

2. Make Fresh Tomatoes and Herbs Sauce, omitting the basil and oregano
   and adding chopped onions and cinnamon. Pour sauce over chicken;
   heat to boiling. Reduce heat and simmer, covered, until chicken is very
   tender, about 45 minutes.

3. Spoon chicken and sauce over linguine.

Nutritional Data

PER SERVING		EXCHANGES	
Calories	358	Milk	0.0
% Calories from fat	22	Veg.	2.0
Fat (gm)	9.1	Fruit	0.0
Sat. Fat (gm)	1.5	Bread	2.5
Cholesterol (mg)	46	Meat	2.0
Sodium (mg)	243	Fat	0.5
Protein (gm)	23.4		
Carbohydrate (gm)	48		

VEAL SAUTE WITH ZITI AND GREMOLATA

Gremolata is a fresh-flavored mixture of finely chopped parsley, lemon rind, and garlic.

8 Servings

Olive oil cooking spray
1½ pounds veal round steak, visible fat trimmed, cut into ½-inch cubes
½ cup chopped onions
2 cans (14½ ounces each) diced tomatoes with Italian seasoning, undrained
Salt and pepper, to taste
1 pound ziti, *or* penne, cooked
Gremolata (recipe follows)

1. Spray large skillet with cooking spray; heat over medium heat until hot. Saute veal and onions until veal is browned, 3 to 5 minutes; remove from skillet.

2. Add tomatoes to skillet and heat to boiling; reduce heat and simmer, uncovered, until thickened, about 10 minutes. Season to taste with salt and pepper. Return veal to skillet, stir and cook 1 to 2 minutes.

3. Toss pasta with tomato sauce and half the Gremolata; serve with remaining Gremolata for passing.

Gremolata

About ½ cup

1 cup packed parsley
1 to 2 tablespoons grated lemon rind
4 large cloves garlic, minced

1. Process all ingredients in food processor until garlic is finely minced, using pulse technique. Refrigerate until ready to use.

Nutritional Data

PER SERVING		EXCHANGES	
Calories	376	Milk	0.0
% Calories from fat	13	Veg.	1.0
Fat (gm)	5.5	Fruit	0.0
Sat. fat (gm)	1.3	Bread	2.5
Cholesterol (mg)	74.6	Meat	3.0
Sodium (mg)	402	Fat	0.0
Protein (gm)	29.1		
Carbohydrate (gm)	51		

WHITEFISH AND LINGUINE WITH LEMON-CAPER SAUCE

Any white-fleshed fish, such as cod, halibut, haddock, or orange roughy, can be used.

6 Servings

6 small whitefish fillets (about 3 ounces each)
1 tablespoon Dijon-style mustard
2 cloves garlic, minced
1 teaspoon dried tarragon leaves
2 tablespoons margarine
3 tablespoons flour
1 can (14½ ounces) low-salt chicken broth
2 to 3 teaspoons lemon juice
3 tablespoons drained capers
¼ teaspoon salt
⅛ teaspoon ground white pepper
12 ounces linguine, cooked, warm

1. Heat oven to 350° F. Brush tops of whitefish fillets with combined mustard, garlic, and tarragon. Place in baking pan; bake until fish is tender and flakes with fork, 10 to 12 minutes.

2. Melt margarine in small saucepan; stir in flour. Cook over medium heat, stirring constantly, 1 to 2 minutes. Stir in chicken broth and lemon juice; heat to boiling. Boil, stirring constantly, until thickened, 1 to 2 minutes. Stir in capers, salt, and pepper.

3. Arrange fish on linguine on serving platter; spoon lemon-caper sauce over fish.

Nutritional Data

PER SERVING		EXCHANGES	
Calories	299	Milk	0.0
% Calories from fat	20	Veg.	0.0
Fat (gm)	6.8	Fruit	0.0
Sat. Fat (gm)	0.9	Bread	2.5
Cholesterol (mg)	34	Meat	2.0
Sodium (mg)	356	Fat	0.0
Protein (gm)	23		
Carbohydrate (gm)	37		

SPINACH GNOCCHI AND CHICKEN PRIMAVERA

Gnocchi, or dumplings, are often made from potatoes.
This spinach version is a delicious variation.

6 Servings

Vegetable cooking spray
1/2 cup chopped onions
2 cloves garlic, minced
3 packages (10 ounces each) frozen chopped
   spinach, thawed
2/3 cup all-purpose flour
1 cup reduced-fat ricotta cheese
1/2 cup grated Parmesan cheese
1 egg
1/4 teaspoon ground nutmeg
1/2 teaspoon salt (optional)
1/2 teaspoon pepper
1/4 cup all-purpose flour
1 1/4 pounds boneless, skinless chicken breasts,
   baked, sliced
   Primavera Sauce (see pg. 76)

1. Spray large skillet with cooking spray; heat over medium heat until hot. Saute onions and garlic until tender, about 5 minutes. Stir in spinach. Cook over medium heat until spinach mixture is quite dry, about 8 minutes, stirring frequently.

2. Stir 2/3 cup flour into spinach. Stir in cheeses, egg, nutmeg, salt, and pepper; cool. Drop 2 tablespoons spinach mixture into 1/4 cup flour; roll into ball. Repeat with remaining spinach mixture, making 18 gnocchi.

3. Heat 3 quarts water to boiling in large saucepan. Add gnocchi to saucepan. Reduce heat and simmer, uncovered, until gnocchi float to surface, about 10 minutes.

4. Arrange chicken and gnocchi on serving platter; spoon Primavera Sauce over.

Nutritional Data

PER SERVING		EXCHANGES	
Calories	464	Milk	0.0
% Calories from fat	30	Veg.	4.0
Fat (gm)	15.8	Fruit	0.0
Sat. Fat (gm)	5.5	Bread	1.5
Cholesterol (mg)	105.2	Meat	4.0
Sodium (mg)	664	Fat	1.0
Protein (gm)	40		
Carbohydrate (gm)	41.6		

CHICKEN AND FETTUCCINE ALFREDO

An old favorite, updated the "skinny" way.

6 Servings

6 small, boneless, skinless chicken breast halves
   (about 3 ounces each)
2 cloves garlic, minced
   Paprika
   Alfredo Sauce (see pg. 73)
1 tablespoon finely chopped fresh basil leaves,
   or 1 teaspoon dried
12 ounces fettuccine, cooked, warm

1. Heat oven to 350° F. Rub chicken with garlic; sprinkle generously with paprika. Place chicken in baking pan and bake until juices run clear, about 35 minutes.

2. Make Alfredo Sauce, adding basil. Spoon Alfredo Sauce over fettuccine and toss. Top with chicken breasts.

Nutritional Data

PER SERVING		EXCHANGES	
Calories	380	Milk	0.5
% Calories from fat	26	Veg.	0.0
Fat (gm)	11	Fruit	0.0
Sat. Fat (gm)	2.6	Bread	2.5
Cholesterol (mg)	48.4	Meat	2.0
Sodium (mg)	506	Fat	1.0
Protein (gm)	29.2		
Carbohydrate (gm)	41.4		

PASTA SANTA FE

Flavors of the Southwest, picante with poblano peppers. If poblano peppers are not available, substitute green bell peppers and add a finely chopped jalapeño pepper to the onions when sauteing.

4 Servings

1 medium onion, sliced
3 cloves garlic, minced
2 tablespoons vegetable oil
2 medium zucchini, sliced
2 medium tomatoes, cut into wedges
2 poblano peppers, sliced
1 cup fresh or frozen, thawed whole kernel corn
2 tablespoons chili powder
1 teaspoon dried oregano leaves
1/2 teaspoon ground cumin
2 tablespoons minced cilantro, *or* parsley
1/2 teaspoon salt
1/4 teaspoon pepper
8 ounces trio maliano (combination of corkscrews, shells, and rigatoni), cooked, warm

1. Saute onions and garlic in oil in large skillet until tender, about 5 minutes. Add remaining vegetables, chili powder, oregano, and cumin. Cook, uncovered, over medium to medium-low heat until vegetables are crisp-tender, 12 to 15 minutes. Stir in cilantro, salt, and pepper.

2. Spoon vegetable mixture over pasta and toss.

Nutritional Data

PER SERVING		EXCHANGES	
Calories	350	Milk	0.0
% Calories from fat	24	Veg.	2.0
Fat (gm)	9.6	Fruit	0.0
Sat. Fat (gm)	1.2	Bread	3.0
Cholesterol (mg)	0	Meat	0.0
Sodium (mg)	327	Fat	2.0
Protein (gm)	11.6		
Carbohydrate (gm)	58		

PASTA WITH GOAT'S CHEESE AND ONION CONFIT

*Try this pasta with flavored specialty pastas,
such as dried mushroom, herb, or black pepper.*

4 Servings

Olive oil cooking spray
4 cups thinly sliced onions
1 teaspoon minced garlic
1/2 teaspoon dried sage leaves
1/2 teaspoon dried rosemary leaves
1 teaspoon sugar
1/2 cup dry white wine, *or* skim milk
2 ounces fat-free cream cheese
2 ounces goat's cheese
Salt and white pepper, to taste
8 ounces whole wheat, *or* plain, thin spaghetti, cooked
2 to 3 tablespoons coarsely chopped walnuts
Sage or rosemary sprigs, as garnish

1. Spray large skillet with cooking spray; heat over medium heat until hot. Add onions; cook, covered, over medium-low to low heat until onions are very soft, about 30 minutes.

2. Stir garlic, sage, rosemary, and sugar into onions; cook, uncovered, over medium-low to low heat until onions are caramelized and brown, 15 to 20 minutes. Stir in wine; simmer 2 to 3 minutes longer. Stir in cream cheese; cook over low heat, stirring, until melted.

3. Remove from heat. Crumble goat's cheese over top and toss. Season to taste with salt and white pepper.

4. Toss pasta and onion mixture on serving platter. Sprinkle with walnuts and garnish with herb sprigs.

Nutritional Data

PER SERVING		EXCHANGES	
Calories	395	Milk	0.0
% Calories from fat	15	Veg.	2.0
Fat (gm)	6.7	Fruit	0.0
Sat. fat (gm)	2.4	Bread	4.0
Cholesterol (mg)	6.5	Meat	0.5
Sodium (mg)	144	Fat	0.5
Protein (gm)	16		
Carbohydrate (gm)	66.9		

LINGUINE WITH FENNEL AND SUN-DRIED TOMATO PESTO

Fennel, or anise, lends a fragrant flavor to this light pasta entree.

6 Servings

Olive oil cooking spray
1 cup thinly sliced onions
1 bulb fennel, thinly sliced
¼ cup dry white wine, *or* water
Sun-Dried Tomato Pesto (see pg. 84)
12 ounces linguine, *or* angel hair pasta, cooked
Fennel tops, as garnish

1. Spray large skillet with cooking spray; heat over medium heat until hot. Add onions and fennel and saute 2 to 3 minutes. Cook, covered, over medium-low heat until onions are very soft, 10 to 15 minutes. Stir in wine and simmer, covered, 15 to 20 minutes or until wine is almost gone.

2. Spoon onion mixture and Sun-Dried Tomato Pesto over pasta in serving bowl and toss; garnish with fennel tops.

Nutritional Data

PER SERVING		EXCHANGES	
Calories	268	Milk	0.0
% Calories from fat	29	Veg.	2.0
Fat (gm)	9	Fruit	0.0
Sat. fat (gm)	0.9	Bread	2.0
Cholesterol (mg)	0	Meat	0.0
Sodium (mg)	209	Fat	1.5
Protein (gm)	9.4		
Carbohydrate (gm)	38.1		

TAGLIATELLE WITH CHICKEN LIVER SAUCE

There are interesting counterpoints of flavor
and texture in this savory pasta dish.

4 Servings

4 ounces chicken livers, cleaned
Flour
2 teaspoons olive oil
2 medium onions, sliced
3 cloves garlic, minced
2 teaspoons dried sage leaves
2 cups julienne carrots
2 medium tart apples, cored, sliced
1½ cups canned low-salt chicken broth
½ cup dry white wine, *or* low-salt chicken broth
1 tablespoon tomato paste
¼ teaspoon salt
⅛ teaspoon pepper
8 ounces flat pasta (tagliatelle or fettuccine),
cooked, warm

1. Coat chicken livers lightly with flour. Saute in oil in medium skillet until tender and no longer pink in center, about 8 minutes. Remove livers from skillet.

2. Add onions, garlic, and sage to skillet; saute until tender, about 5 minutes. Return livers to skillet. Add carrots, apples, chicken broth, and wine. Heat to boiling. Reduce heat and simmer, uncovered, until vegetables are crisp-tender and sauce thickened, about 15 minutes. Stir in tomato paste, salt, and pepper; cook 2 to 3 minutes more.

3. Serve chicken liver mixture over pasta.

Nutritional Data

PER SERVING		EXCHANGES	
Calories	368	Milk	0.0
% Calories from fat	14	Veg.	3.0
Fat (gm)	5.8	Fruit	1.0
Sat. Fat (gm)	0.9	Bread	3.0
Cholesterol (mg)	110.8	Meat	0.5
Sodium (mg)	250	Fat	0.5
Protein (gm)	15.2		
Carbohydrate (gm)	60.4		

FETTUCCINE WITH PORK, GREENS, AND CARAMELIZED ONIONS

Cooked chicken breast or shrimp would be delicious alternatives to the pork in this recipe.

4 Servings

 4 medium onions, sliced
 1 tablespoon olive oil
 1 teaspoon sugar
 2 cans (14 1/2 ounces each) low-salt chicken broth
 2 cups thinly sliced kale, *or* mustard greens, *or* Swiss chard
 2 cups thinly sliced curly endive, *or* spinach
 1/4 teaspoon salt
 1/4 teaspoon pepper
   Olive oil cooking spray
 12 ounces lean pork tenderloin, fat trimmed, cut into 1/4-inch slices
 8 ounces fettuccine, cooked, warm

1. Cook onions in oil over medium heat in large skillet 5 minutes; reduce heat to low and stir in sugar. Cook until onions are golden in color and very soft, about 20 minutes.

2. Stir chicken broth into onions; heat to boiling. Reduce heat and simmer, uncovered, until broth is reduced by 1/3, about 10 minutes. Add greens; simmer, covered, until greens are wilted, 5 to 7 minutes. Simmer, uncovered, until broth is almost absorbed by greens, about 5 minutes. Stir in salt and pepper.

3. Spray large skillet with cooking spray; heat over medium heat until hot. Cook pork slices over medium to medium-high heat until browned and no longer pink in center, about 5 minutes.

4. Spoon onion mixture over pasta and toss; add pork and toss.

Nutritional Data

PER SERVING		EXCHANGES	
Calories	389	Milk	0.0
% Calories from fat	22	Veg.	3.0
Fat (gm)	9.6	Fruit	0.0
Sat. Fat (gm)	1.6	Bread	2.5
Cholesterol (mg)	60.5	Meat	2.0
Sodium (mg)	345	Fat	0.5
Protein (gm)	30.5		
Carbohydrate (gm)	46.9		

RIGATONI WITH ITALIAN SAUSAGE AND FENNEL PESTO

Italian and smoked sausages are now being made with "skinnier" ground turkey. Turkey sausage is sold in bulk form and sometimes in links.

6 Servings

1 pound smoked turkey Italian sausage (bulk or links)
1½ cups thinly sliced fennel bulb, *or* celery
1 cup chopped onions
2 cloves garlic, minced
1 can (8 ounces) low-sodium whole tomatoes, drained, chopped
Fennel Pesto (recipe follows)
12 ounces rigatoni, *or* other tube pasta, cooked, warm

1. Cook sausage in large skillet over medium heat until browned, 8 to 10 minutes. Remove sausage from skillet and drain on paper toweling; drain excess fat from skillet. If using sausage links, slice into ½-inch pieces.

2. Add fennel, onions, and garlic to skillet; saute until onions are transparent. Stir in tomatoes and sausage; stir in Fennel Pesto. Heat to boiling; reduce heat and simmer, covered, about 15 minutes.

3. Spoon sauce mixture over pasta and toss.

Fennel Pesto

Makes about 1 1/3 cups

1 tablespoon fennel seeds
  Hot water
1 cup chopped fennel bulb, *or* celery
1/2 cup parsley, loosely packed
2 cloves garlic
14 walnut halves (about 1 ounce)
3 tablespoons water
1 tablespoon olive oil
1/4 cup grated Parmesan cheese

1. Place fennel seeds in small bowl; pour hot water over to cover. Let stand 10 minutes; drain.

2. Process fennel, fennel seeds, parsley, and garlic in food processor or blender until finely chopped. Add walnuts, 3 tablespoons water, and oil; process until walnuts are finely chopped. Stir in Parmesan cheese.

Nutritional Data

PER SERVING		EXCHANGES	
Calories	406	Milk	0.0
% Calories from fat	29	Veg.	1.0
Fat (gm)	13	Fruit	0.0
Sat. Fat (gm)	2.9	Bread	2.5
Cholesterol (mg)	48.2	Meat	2.0
Sodium (mg)	711	Fat	2.0
Protein (gm)	24.6		
Carbohydrate (gm)	48.3		

CHICKEN FRICASSEE WITH PAPPARDELLE

For special occasions, add a festive note to this recipe by substituting ¹/₂ cup dry sherry or white wine for ¹/₂ cup of the chicken broth.

6 Servings

Vegetable cooking spray
1¹/₄ pounds boneless, skinless chicken breasts, cut into ¹/₂-inch strips
1 medium onion, cut into wedges
4 medium carrots, cut into 1-inch pieces
4 ribs celery, cut into 1-inch pieces
2 cloves garlic, minced
3 tablespoons flour
2 cans (14¹/₂ ounces each) low-salt chicken broth
16 whole cloves
2 bay leaves
1 teaspoon lemon juice
¹/₂ teaspoon sugar
¹/₂ teaspoon salt
¹/₄ teaspoon pepper
12 ounces pappardelle, *or* other wide, flat pasta, cooked, warm
1 tablespoon minced parsley

1. Spray Dutch oven or large skillet with cooking spray; heat over medium heat until hot. Cook chicken until no longer pink in center, about 8 minutes. Remove chicken from pot.

2. Add vegetables to pot; saute 5 minutes. Stir in flour; cook 1 to 2 minutes. Return chicken to pot; add chicken broth; cloves and bay leaves tied in cheesecloth; lemon juice; and sugar. Heat to boiling. Reduce heat and simmer, covered, 10 minutes. Simmer, uncovered, until sauce is medium consistency, about 10 minutes. Discard spice packet; stir in salt and pepper.

3. Spoon chicken mixture over pasta and toss; sprinkle with parsley.

Nutritional Data

PER SERVING		EXCHANGES	
Calories	349	Milk	0.0
% Calories from fat	11	Veg.	1.0
Fat (gm)	4.2	Fruit	0.0
Sat. Fat (gm)	0.8	Bread	3.0
Cholesterol (mg)	48.5	Meat	2.0
Sodium (mg)	287	Fat	0.0
Protein (gm)	28		
Carbohydrate (gm)	48.4		

FETTUCCINE WITH CHICKEN PICCATA

This "skinny" version of the classic piccata is sure to please.

6 Servings

  6 small boneless, skinless chicken breast halves (about 3 ounces each)
      Flour
      Vegetable cooking spray
  1 tablespoon margarine
  2 tablespoons flour
  1 can (14 1/2 ounces) low-salt chicken broth
 1/2 cup dry white wine, *or* low-salt chicken broth
  2 tablespoons lemon juice
  1 tablespoon finely chopped parsley
  2 teaspoons drained capers (optional)
 12 ounces fettuccine, cooked, warm

1. Pound chicken with flat side of meat mallet to scant 1/4-inch thickness; coat lightly with flour. Spray large skillet with cooking spray; heat over medium heat until hot. Cook chicken over medium to medium-high heat until browned and no longer pink in center, 3 to 5 minutes. Remove chicken from skillet.

2. Melt margarine in skillet; stir in 2 tablespoons flour and cook over medium heat 1 to 2 minutes. Stir in chicken broth, wine, and lemon juice; heat to boiling. Boil, stirring constantly, until slightly thickened, 1 to 2 minutes. Reduce heat and simmer, uncovered, until thickened to medium sauce consistency, about 15 minutes more. Stir in parsley and capers.

3. Return chicken to sauce; cook over medium-low heat until chicken is hot through, 2 to 3 minutes. Serve chicken and sauce over pasta.

Nutritional Data

PER SERVING		EXCHANGES	
Calories	301	Milk	0.0
% Calories from fat	18	Veg.	0.0
Fat (gm)	6	Fruit	0.0
Sat. Fat (gm)	0.9	Bread	2.5
Cholesterol (mg)	43.4	Meat	2.0
Sodium (mg)	175	Fat	0.0
Protein (gm)	24.3		
Carbohydrate (gm)	35		

SALMON WITH CILANTRO PESTO FETTUCCINE

♦

Tuna or halibut can be substituted nicely for the salmon.

6 Servings

1 large salmon fillet (about 12 ounces)
2 teaspoons Dijon-style mustard
12 ounces spinach fettuccine, cooked, warm
Cilantro Pesto (see pg. 83)

1. Brush salmon fillet with mustard; place on broiler pan. Broil, 6 inches from heat source, until salmon is tender and flakes with fork, 10 to 15 minutes.

2. Toss fettuccine with Cilantro Pesto; arrange around salmon on serving platter.

Nutritional Data

PER SERVING		EXCHANGES	
Calories	292	Milk	0.0
% Calories from fat	30	Veg.	0.0
Fat (gm)	10.2	Fruit	0.0
Sat. Fat (gm)	1.5	Bread	2.0
Cholesterol (mg)	13.5	Meat	2.0
Sodium (mg)	323	Fat	1.0
Protein (gm)	19.1		
Carbohydrate (gm)	33.5		

CHICKEN AND CHEESE ROTOLO WITH MANY-CLOVES GARLIC SAUCE

Some people prefer cutting lasagne noodles into halves before filling, as they are easier to handle in eating. If cut, spread each noodle half with 1½ to 2 tablespoons of the cheese mixture.

6 Servings

1 pound boneless, skinless chicken breast, cooked, shredded
1¼ cups reduced-fat ricotta cheese
3 to 4 cloves garlic, minced
¾ teaspoon dried marjoram leaves
½ teaspoon dried thyme leaves
½ teaspoon salt
¼ teaspoon pepper
12 lasagne noodles (10 ounces), cooked, room temperature
Many-Cloves Garlic Sauce (see pg. 78)

1. Mix chicken, cheese, garlic, herbs, salt, and pepper. Spread 3 to 4 tablespoons of mixture evenly on each noodle; roll up and place in baking dish.

2. Heat oven to 350° F. Spoon Many Cloves Garlic Sauce over rotolo. Bake, loosely covered with aluminum foil, until rotolo are hot through and sauce is bubbly, 20 to 30 minutes.

Nutritional Data

PER SERVING		EXCHANGES	
Calories	295	Milk	0.0
% Calories from fat	28	Veg.	1.0
Fat (gm)	9.4	Fruit	0.0
Sat. Fat (gm)	1.1	Bread	1.5
Cholesterol (mg)	45.1	Meat	2.5
Sodium (mg)	315	Fat	0.5
Protein (gm)	23.3		
Carbohydrate (gm)	28.1		

SPINACH-MUSHROOM ROTOLO WITH MARINARA SAUCE

One of the seafood sauces, such as Red Clam Sauce or Cioppino Sauce (see pgs. 58, 67), would be other options for the rotolo.

6 Servings

Olive oil cooking spray
2 cups sliced mushrooms
1 package (10 ounces) fresh spinach, cleaned, chopped
2 cloves garlic, minced
1 teaspoon dried basil leaves
1 teaspoon dried tarragon leaves
1/2 package (8 ounce-size) reduced-fat cream cheese, room temperature
1/2 cup fat-free ricotta cheese
1/4 teaspoon salt
1/4 teaspoon pepper
12 lasagne noodles, cooked, room temperature
Marinara Sauce (see pg. 60)

1. Spray large skillet with cooking spray; heat over medium heat until hot. Cook mushrooms, covered, until they release juices, 3 to 5 minutes. Add spinach, garlic, and herbs to skillet; cook, covered, until spinach is wilted, 2 to 3 minutes. Cook, uncovered, over medium to medium-high heat until liquid is gone, about 10 minutes; cool.

2. Combine cheeses, salt, and pepper in bowl; stir in mushroom mixture. Spread 3 to 4 tablespoons cheese mixture on each noodle; roll up and place in baking dish.

3. Heat oven to 350° F. Spoon Marinara Sauce over rotolo. Bake, loosely covered with aluminum foil, until rotolo are hot through and sauce is bubbly, 20 to 30 minutes.

Nutritional Data

PER SERVING		EXCHANGES	
Calories	286	Milk	0.0
% Calories from fat	30	Veg.	3.0
Fat (gm)	10.3	Fruit	0.0
Sat. Fat (gm)	2.7	Bread	1.5
Cholesterol (mg)	8.7	Meat	0.0
Sodium (mg)	686	Fat	2.0
Protein (gm)	12.5		
Carbohydrate (gm)	38		

VEGGIE LASAGNE WITH EGGPLANT SAUCE

The hearty Eggplant Sauce is also wonderful served over shaped or tube pastas, such as corkscrews or ziti, or over cheese or chicken tortelloni.

8 Servings

Olive oil cooking spray
1 medium onion, sliced
1 medium zucchini, sliced
1 medium red bell pepper, sliced
1 cup sliced mushrooms
3 cloves garlic, minced
2 cups fat-free ricotta cheese
1/4 cup grated Parmesan cheese
Eggplant Sauce (see pg. 70)
12 lasagne noodles (10 ounces), cooked, room temperature
2 medium-size sweet potatoes, sliced, cooked until crisp-tender
2 cups (8 ounces) shredded, reduced-fat mozzarella cheese

1. Spray large skillet with cooking spray; heat over medium heat until hot. Saute onions, zucchini, bell pepper, mushrooms, and garlic until tender, about 10 minutes. In bowl, mix ricotta and Parmesan cheese.

2. Heat oven to 350° F. Spread about 1/2 cup Eggplant Sauce in bottom of 13 x 9-inch baking pan; top with 4 lasagne noodles, overlapping slight-

ly. Spoon ⅓ of ricotta cheese mixture over noodles, spreading lightly with rubber spatula. Add next layer, using ⅓ of sweet potatoes and ⅓ of sauteed vegetables. Spoon ⅓ Eggplant Sauce over vegetables; sprinkle with ⅓ of mozzarella cheese. Repeat layers 2 times.

3. Bake lasagne, loosely covered with aluminum foil, until sauce is bubbly, about 1 hour.

Nutritional Data

PER SERVING		EXCHANGES	
Calories	375	Milk	0.0
% Calories from fat	24	Veg.	3.0
Fat (gm)	10.4	Fruit	0.0
Sat. Fat (gm)	4.2	Bread	2.0
Cholesterol (mg)	23.7	Meat	2.5
Sodium (mg)	685	Fat	0.5
Protein (gm)	24.1		
Carbohydrate (gm)	47		

SAUSAGE LASAGNE

The traditional lasagne we all love, with a "skinny" rendering.

8 Servings

- 2 cups fat-free ricotta cheese
- 1/4 cup grated Parmesan cheese
- 3 cups (12 ounces) shredded, reduced-fat mozzarella cheese
- **Tomato Sauce with Italian Sausage** (recipe follows)
- 12 lasagne noodles (10 ounces), cooked, room temperature

1. Heat oven to 350° F. Combine cheeses in bowl. Spread 1 cup Tomato Sauce on bottom of 13 x 9-inch baking pan; top with 4 lasagne noodles, overlapping slightly. Spoon 1/3 of cheese mixture over noodles, spreading lightly with rubber spatula. Top with 1 cup Tomato Sauce. Repeat layers 2 times, ending with layer of noodles, cheese, and remaining Tomato Sauce.

2. Bake lasagne, loosely covered with aluminum foil, until sauce is bubbly, about 1 hour.

Tomato Sauce with Italian Sausage

Makes about 4 1/2 cups

- Olive oil cooking spray
- 2 cups chopped onions
- 3 cloves garlic, minced
- 1 teaspoon dried basil leaves
- 1 teaspoon dried tarragon leaves
- 1 teaspoon dried thyme leaves
- 2 cans (16 ounces each) low-sodium whole tomatoes, undrained, coarsely chopped
- 2 cans (8 ounces each) low-sodium tomato sauce
- 1 cup water
- 1 to 2 teaspoons sugar
- 8 ounces turkey Italian sausage, cooked, well drained
- 1/4 teaspoon salt
- 1/4 teaspoon pepper

1. Spray large saucepan with cooking spray; heat over medium heat until hot. Saute onions and garlic until tender, about 5 minutes; stir in herbs and cook 1 to 2 minutes more.

2. Add tomatoes, tomato sauce, and water; heat to boiling. Reduce heat and simmer, uncovered, until sauce is reduced to about 4½ cups, 15 to 20 minutes. Stir in sugar; stir in sausage, salt, and pepper.

Nutritional Data

PER SERVING		EXCHANGES	
Calories	375	Milk	0.0
% Calories from fat	30	Veg.	2.5
Fat (gm)	12.9	Fruit	0.0
Sat. Fat (gm)	6	Bread	1.5
Cholesterol (mg)	47.3	Meat	3.5
Sodium (mg)	679	Fat	0.5
Protein (gm)	31.3		
Carbohydrate (gm)	33.9		

MEXICAN-STYLE LASAGNE

A lasagne with a difference—olé!

8 Servings

2 cups fat-free ricotta cheese
2 cups shredded, reduced-fat Monterey Jack cheese
1 can (15 ounces) pinto beans, drained
1 can (15 ounces) black beans, drained
Chili-Tomato Sauce (recipe follows)
12 lasagne noodles (10 ounces), cooked, room temperature
1/4 cup finely chopped cilantro, *or* parsley

1. Heat oven to 350° F. Combine ricotta and Monterey Jack cheese. Combine pinto and black beans. Spread 1 1/2 cups Chili-Tomato Sauce on bottom of 13 x 9-inch baking pan; top with 4 lasagne noodles, overlapping slightly. Spoon 1/3 of cheese mixture over noodles, spreading lightly with rubber spatula; top with 1/3 of beans and 1 cup Chili-Tomato Sauce. Repeat layers 2 times, ending with remaining 1 1/2 cups sauce.

2. Bake lasagne, loosely covered with aluminum foil, until sauce is bubbly, about 1 hour. Sprinkle with cilantro before serving.

Chili-Tomato Sauce

Makes about 5 cups

Olive oil cooking spray
2 cups chopped onions
3 cloves garlic, minced
2 to 3 teaspoons minced jalapeño peppers
2 cans (14 1/2 ounces each) low-sodium stewed tomatoes
2 cans (8 ounces each) low-sodium tomato sauce
2 tablespoons chili powder
2 teaspoons ground cumin
1 teaspoon dried oregano leaves
1/4 to 1/2 teaspoon salt

1. Spray large saucepan with cooking spray; heat over medium heat until hot. Saute onions, garlic, and jalapeño peppers until onions are tender, 5 to 8 minutes.

2. Stir in remaining ingredients, except salt; heat to boiling. Reduce heat and simmer, uncovered, until sauce is reduced to 5 cups, about 20 minutes. Stir in salt.

Nutritional Data

PER SERVING		EXCHANGES	
Calories	360	Milk	0.0
% Calories from fat	18	Veg.	3.0
Fat (gm)	8	Fruit	0.0
Sat. Fat (gm)	3.1	Bread	2.0
Cholesterol (mg)	26.3	Meat	2.5
Sodium (mg)	748	Fat	0.5
Protein (gm)	30.7		
Carbohydrate (gm)	51		

SHRIMP AND ARTICHOKE RAVIOLI WITH TARRAGON SAUCE

◆

Red Pepper Sauce or Tomatoes and Herbs Sauce (see pgs. 81, 62) would also be flavorful sauce selections for the ravioli.

4 Servings (4 ravioli each)

Olive oil cooking spray
8 ounces finely chopped, peeled, deveined shrimp
1 can (or jar) artichoke hearts, drained, rinsed, finely chopped
1 clove garlic, minced
¼ teaspoon ground nutmeg
3 tablespoons dry white wine, *or* water
32 wonton wrappers
Water
Tarragon Sauce (recipe follows)

1. Spray large skillet with cooking spray; heat over medium heat until hot. Add shrimp, artichoke hearts, garlic, nutmeg, and wine. Cook over medium heat until shrimp are cooked and liquid is gone, about 5 minutes. Cool.

2. Place about 2 teaspoons shrimp mixture on wonton wrapper; brush edges of wrapper with water. Top with second wonton wrapper and press edges together to seal. Repeat with remaining wonton wrappers and shrimp mixture.

3. Heat about 2 quarts water to boiling in large saucepan; add 4 to 6 ravioli. Reduce heat and simmer, uncovered, until ravioli float to surface and are *al dente*, 3 to 4 minutes. Remove ravioli with slotted spoon; repeat cooking procedure with remaining ravioli. Serve with Tarragon Sauce.

Tarragon Sauce

Makes about 1 cup

2   medium shallots, finely chopped
1   tablespoon finely chopped fresh tarragon leaves, *or* 1/2 teaspoon dried
1/2 cup dry white wine, *or* canned low-salt chicken broth
1   cup canned low-salt chicken broth, divided
1   tablespoon flour
1/4 teaspoon salt
1/8 teaspoon ground white pepper

1. Heat shallots, tarragon, and wine to boiling in small saucepan; reduce heat and simmer, uncovered, until mixture is reduced to 1/4 cup.

2. Add 1/2 cup chicken broth; heat to boiling. Mix flour and remaining 1/2 cup chicken broth; stir into boiling mixture. Boil until thickened (sauce will be thin), stirring constantly. Stir in salt and pepper.

Nutritional Data

PER SERVING		EXCHANGES	
Calories	331	Milk	0.0
% Calories from fat	5	Veg.	2.0
Fat (gm)	1.9	Fruit	0.0
Sat. Fat (gm)	0.4	Bread	3.0
Cholesterol (mg)	95.1	Meat	1.0
Sodium (mg)	719	Fat	0.0
Protein (gm)	20.4		
Carbohydrate (gm)	53		

CHICKEN AND SWEET POTATO RAVIOLI WITH CURRY SAUCE

The light curry-flavored sauce is a delicate accompaniment to this unusual ravioli.

4 Servings (4 ravioli each)

8 ounces boneless, skinless chicken breast, baked, shredded
1 cup mashed sweet potatoes
2 small cloves garlic, minced
1/2 to 3/4 teaspoon ground ginger
1/4 teaspoon salt
1/4 teaspoon ground white pepper
32 wonton wrappers
Water
Curry Sauce (recipe follows)

1. Mix chicken, sweet potatoes, garlic, ginger, salt, and pepper. Spoon about 2 teaspoons chicken mixture onto wonton wrapper; brush edges of wrapper with water. Top with second wonton wrapper and press edges together to seal. Repeat with remaining wonton wrappers and chicken mixture.

2. Heat about 2 quarts water to boiling in large saucepan; add 4 to 6 ravioli. Reduce heat and simmer, uncovered, until ravioli float to surface and are *al dente,* 3 to 4 minutes. Remove ravioli with slotted spoon; repeat cooking procedure with remaining ravioli. Serve with Curry Sauce.

Curry Sauce

Makes about 1 cup

2 tablespoons finely chopped onions
2 cloves garlic, minced
1 tablespoon margarine
1 tablespoon flour
2 teaspoons curry powder
1/8 teaspoon cayenne pepper
1 cup canned low-salt chicken broth
2 to 4 tablespoons dry white wine (optional)

1. Saute onions and garlic in margarine in small saucepan 2 to 3 minutes; stir in flour, curry powder, and pepper. Cook 1 minute more, stirring constantly.

2. Stir chicken broth and wine into saucepan; heat to boiling. Boil until sauce is thickened (sauce will be thin), stirring constantly.

Nutritional Data

PER SERVING		EXCHANGES	
Calories	383	Milk	0.0
% Calories from fat	13	Veg.	0.5
Fat (gm)	5.5	Fruit	0.0
Sat. Fat (gm)	1.1	Bread	4.0
Cholesterol (mg)	37.2	Meat	1.5
Sodium (mg)	587	Fat	0.0
Protein (gm)	19.8		
Carbohydrate (gm)	62.4		

TURKEY AND HERBED-CHEESE RAVIOLI WITH WILD MUSHROOM SAUCE

◆

Reduced-fat turkey Italian sausage can be used nicely in these ravioli.

4 Servings (4 ravioli each)

Olive oil cooking spray
8 ounces ground turkey
1 small onion, minced
2 cloves garlic, minced
1 cup reduced-fat ricotta cheese
1 teaspoon dried rosemary leaves
32 wonton wrappers
Water
Wild Mushroom Sauce (see pg. 80)

1. Spray small skillet with cooking spray; heat over medium heat until hot. Cook turkey over medium heat until browned, about 5 minutes; drain on paper toweling. Discard fat from skillet. Add onions and garlic and saute until onion is tender, about 5 minutes.

2. Mix in ricotta cheese and rosemary; mix in turkey. Place about 2 teaspoons mixture on wonton wrapper; brush edges of wrapper with water. Top with a second wonton wrapper and press edges together to seal. Repeat with remaining wonton wrappers and turkey mixture.

3. Heat about 2 quarts water to boiling in large saucepan; add 4 to 6 ravioli. Reduce heat and simmer, uncovered, until ravioli float to surface and are *al dente,* 3 to 4 minutes. Repeat cooking procedure with remaining ravioli. Serve with Wild Mushroom Sauce.

Nutritional Data

PER SERVING		EXCHANGES	
Calories	360	Milk	0.0
% Calories from fat	18	Veg.	1.5
Fat (gm)	7.2	Fruit	0.0
Sat. Fat (gm)	1.4	Bread	3.0
Cholesterol (mg)	37	Meat	1.5
Sodium (mg)	593	Fat	0.5
Protein (gm)	22		
Carbohydrate (gm)	53		

CHICKEN AND PASTA MARENGO

The orange-scented tomato sauce, subtly seasoned with herbs and wine, benefits from day-ahead preparation, giving flavors an opportunity to meld.

6 Servings

- 6 small boneless, skinless chicken breast halves (about 3 ounces each)
  Flour
- 1 tablespoon olive oil
- 1 small onion, chopped
- 3 cloves garlic, minced
- 1 can (14 1/2 ounces) low-salt chicken broth
- 1/2 cup dry white wine, *or* canned low-salt chicken broth
- 3 tablespoons tomato paste
- 2 tablespoons grated orange peel
- 1 teaspoon dried tarragon leaves
- 1 teaspoon dried thyme leaves
- 2 cups sliced mushrooms
- 1/4 teaspoon salt (optional)
- 1/4 teaspoon pepper
- 12 ounces pappardelle, *or* other wide, flat pasta, cooked, warm

1. Coat chicken breasts lightly with flour. Saute in oil in Dutch oven until browned, about 4 minutes each side. Remove chicken. Add onions and garlic to Dutch oven; saute until tender, 3 to 4 minutes.

2. Heat oven to 325° F. Add chicken broth, wine, tomato paste, orange peel, and herbs to Dutch oven; heat to boiling. Add chicken and bake, loosely covered, until chicken is tender, 45 to 60 minutes, adding mushrooms during last 15 to 20 minutes of cooking time. Stir in salt and pepper.

3. Spoon about 2/3 of sauce over pasta on serving platter and toss. Arrange chicken on pasta and spoon remaining sauce over.

Nutritional Data

PER SERVING		EXCHANGES	
Calories	343	Milk	0.0
% Calories from fat	16	Veg.	1.0
Fat (gm)	6.1	Fruit	0.0
Sat. Fat (gm)	1.1	Bread	2.5
Cholesterol (mg)	43.5	Meat	2.5
Sodium (mg)	133	Fat	0.0
Protein (gm)	25.4		
Carbohydrate (gm)	42.7		

CHICKEN-STUFFED SHELLS WITH WHITE SAUCE

Purchased ground chicken or turkey breast can be used in this dish, though the texture of the filling is better if prepared according to the recipe. Cook the shells for the minimum time indicated so that they are al dente.

6 Servings (5 shells each)

1 pound boneless, skinless chicken breast
1 cup skim milk
1 egg white
1½ to 2 tablespoons fennel seeds, crushed
3 cloves garlic, minced
1 teaspoon dried rosemary leaves
¼ teaspoon ground nutmeg
¼ teaspoon salt
¼ teaspoon pepper
3 to 4 dashes red pepper sauce
30 jumbo shells (9 ounces), cooked, room temperature
White Sauce (recipe follows)
Parsley, finely chopped

1. Process chicken breast in the food processor, using on/off technique, until very finely chopped. Add remaining ingredients, except pasta, White Sauce, and parsley; process just until blended.

2. Heat oven to 350° F. Spoon mixture into shells and arrange in lightly greased baking pan; spoon White Sauce over shells. Bake, loosely covered, until filling is cooked and begins to pull away from edges of shells, 30 to 35 minutes. Sprinkle with parsley.

White Sauce

Makes about 2 cups

- 1 tablespoon margarine
- 2 tablespoons flour
- 2 cups skim milk
- ¼ cup grated Parmesan cheese
- ⅛ teaspoon ground white pepper

1. Melt margarine in medium saucepan; stir in flour. Cook over medium heat, stirring constantly, 1 to 2 minutes.

2. Add milk to saucepan; heat to boiling, stirring frequently. Boil, stirring constantly, until thickened, 1 to 2 minutes (sauce will still be very thin).

3. Remove saucepan from heat; stir in cheese and pepper.

Nutritional Data

PER SERVING		EXCHANGES	
Calories	321	Milk	0.5
% Calories from fat	18	Veg.	0.0
Fat (gm)	6.5	Fruit	0.0
Sat. Fat (gm)	2	Bread	2.0
Cholesterol (mg)	43.8	Meat	2.5
Sodium (mg)	302	Fat	0.0
Protein (gm)	27		
Carbohydrate (gm)	37.4		

CHICKEN-VEGETABLE MANICOTTI WITH CREAMED SPINACH SAUCE

Three-Onion Sauce and Tomato Sauce with Mushrooms and Sherry (see pgs. 77, 61) are also excellent accompaniments for the manicotti.

4 Servings (3 manicotti each)

Olive oil cooking spray
1/2 cup chopped onions
3 cloves garlic, minced
2 cups spinach leaves, chopped
1/2 cup chopped zucchini
1/2 cup chopped yellow summer squash
1 teaspoon dried basil leaves
1 teaspoon dried oregano leaves
8 ounces boneless, skinless chicken, cooked, finely shredded
1/2 cup reduced-fat ricotta cheese
1/4 teaspoon salt
1/4 teaspoon pepper
1 package (8 ounces) manicotti, cooked, room temperature
Creamed Spinach Sauce (see pg. 75)

1. Spray large skillet with cooking spray; heat over medium heat until hot. Saute onions and garlic until tender, about 3 minutes. Add remaining vegetables; saute until tender, 5 to 8 minutes. Stir in herbs and cook 2 minutes more. Stir in chicken, cheese, salt, and pepper.

2. Heat oven to 350° F. Spoon about 3 tablespoons chicken-vegetable mixture into each manicotti; arrange in baking pan. Spoon Creamed Spinach Sauce over manicotti. Bake, loosely covered with aluminum foil, until manicotti are hot through and sauce is bubbly, 35 to 40 minutes.

Nutritional Data

PER SERVING		EXCHANGES	
Calories	510	Milk	0.5
% Calories from fat	24	Veg.	3.0
Fat (gm)	13.7	Fruit	0.0
Sat. Fat (gm)	4	Bread	3.0
Cholesterol (mg)	46.6	Meat	1.5
Sodium (mg)	640	Fat	2.0
Protein (gm)	34.5		
Carbohydrate (gm)	65.2		

MUSHROOM-BROCCOLI MANICOTTI

Any pasta that is going to be filled and baked should be cooked only until al dente so that the completed dish is not overcooked.

4 Servings (3 manicotti each)

Olive oil cooking spray
4 shallots, *or* green onions, chopped
3 cloves garlic, minced
2 cups sliced mushrooms
2 cups finely chopped, cooked broccoli
2 teaspoons dried basil leaves
1 teaspoon dried marjoram leaves
1 cup reduced-fat ricotta cheese
1/4 teaspoon salt
1/4 teaspoon pepper
1 package (8 ounces) manicotti, cooked, room temperature
Tomato Sauce with Mushrooms and Sherry (see pg. 61)

1. Spray large skillet with cooking spray; heat over medium heat until hot. Saute shallots and garlic until tender, 2 to 3 minutes. Add mushrooms; cook, covered, until mushrooms release juices, 3 to 5 minutes. Cook, uncovered, over medium to medium-high heat, until liquid is gone, about 10 minutes. Stir in broccoli, basil, and marjoram; cook 2 to 3 minutes. Stir in cheese, salt, and pepper.

2. Heat oven to 350° F. Spoon about 3 tablespoons vegetable-cheese mixture into each manicotti; arrange in baking pan. Spoon Tomato Sauce

with Mushrooms and Sherry over manicotti. Bake, loosely covered with aluminum foil, until manicotti are hot through and sauce is bubbly, 30 to 35 minutes.

Nutritional Data

PER SERVING		EXCHANGES	
Calories	394	Milk	0.0
% Calories from fat	17	Veg.	4.0
Fat (gm)	7.8	Fruit	0.0
Sat. Fat (gm)	0.8	Bread	3.0
Cholesterol (mg)	7.9	Meat	0.0
Sodium (mg)	665	Fat	1.5
Protein (gm)	19.2		
Carbohydrate (gm)	63.4		

TURKEY TETRAZZINI

This dish was named for the famous Italian opera singer, Lucia Tetrazzini, who claimed it as her favorite.

8 Servings

 8 ounces mushrooms, sliced
 2 tablespoons margarine
 2 tablespoons flour
 1 can (14 1/2 ounces) low-salt chicken broth
 1 cup skim milk
 1/2 cup dry white wine, *or* skim milk
 16 ounces spaghettini (thin spaghetti)
 12 ounces boneless, skinless turkey, cooked, cubed, *or* chicken breast
 1/4 cup grated Parmesan cheese
 1/4 teaspoon ground nutmeg
 1/4 teaspoon salt
 1/4 teaspoon pepper

1. Saute mushrooms in margarine in large saucepan until tender, about 5 minutes. Stir in flour; cook over medium heat 1 to 2 minutes more. Stir in chicken broth, milk, and wine and heat to boiling. Boil, stirring constantly, until thickened, 1 to 2 minutes (sauce will be very thin). Stir in pasta, turkey, Parmesan cheese, nutmeg, salt, and pepper.

2. Heat oven to 350° F. Spoon pasta mixture into 2-quart casserole or baking dish. Bake, uncovered, until lightly browned on top and bubbly, about 45 minutes.

Nutritional Data

PER SERVING		EXCHANGES	
Calories	370	Milk	0.0
% Calories from fat	16	Veg.	1.0
Fat (gm)	6.5	Fruit	0.0
Sat. Fat (gm)	1.7	Bread	3.0
Cholesterol (mg)	35.7	Meat	2.0
Sodium (mg)	218	Fat	0.5
Protein (gm)	23.6		
Carbohydrate (gm)	50.3		

MACARONI AND CHEESE

The combination of cheeses contributes the creamy texture and distinctive flavor to this lower-fat version of an all-time favorite.

6 Side-Dish Servings (about ²/₃ cup each)

- ¼ cup finely chopped onions
- 2 tablespoons margarine
- 3 tablespoons flour
- 1 bay leaf
- 2 ½ cups skim milk
- ¾ cup (3 ounces) shredded reduced-fat American cheese
- ¾ cup (3 ounces) shredded reduced-fat Cheddar cheese
- 1 teaspoon Dijon-style mustard
- ¼ teaspoon pepper
- 10 ounces fusilli, *or* rotini (corkscrews), cooked, room temperature
- 2 tablespoons grated Parmesan cheese, *or* dry unseasoned breadcrumbs

1. Saute onions in margarine until tender, 2 to 3 minutes. Stir in flour and bay leaf and cook 1 to 2 minutes, stirring frequently. Stir in milk; heat to boiling. Boil until thickened, stirring constantly (sauce will be thin). Remove from heat; stir in American and Cheddar cheeses, mustard, and pepper.

2. Heat oven to 350° F. Pour sauce over pasta in 1-quart casserole; stir to combine, and sprinkle with Parmesan cheese. Bake, uncovered, until hot through and lightly browned on top, about 30 minutes.

Nutritional Data

PER SERVING		EXCHANGES	
Calories	330	Milk	0.5
% Calories from fat	28	Veg.	0.0
Fat (gm)	10	Fruit	0.0
Sat. Fat (gm)	4	Bread	2.5
Cholesterol (mg)	18.5	Meat	1.0
Sodium (mg)	559	Fat	1.0
Protein (gm)	17.4		
Carbohydrate (gm)	42		

SPAGHETTI AND EGGPLANT PARMESAN

Baked in a springform pan, the presentation of this dish is unusual and quite attractive.

6 Servings

Olive oil cooking spray
1 large eggplant (about 3 pounds), sliced 1/4-inch thick
1 small onion, very finely chopped
3 cloves garlic, minced
1 tablespoon olive oil
2 cans (8 ounces each) low-sodium tomato sauce
8 medium plum tomatoes, chopped
1/8 teaspoon crushed red pepper
3 tablespoons finely chopped fresh basil leaves, *or* 2 teaspoons dried
12 ounces spaghetti, cooked, room temperature
1/4 cup grated Parmesan cheese
2 to 3 tablespoons dry unseasoned breadcrumbs

1. Spray large skillet with cooking spray; heat over medium heat until hot. Cook eggplant slices until browned, about 4 minutes on each side. Set aside.

2. Saute onions and garlic in oil in large skillet until tender, 3 to 5 minutes. Add tomato sauce, tomatoes, and red pepper to skillet; heat to boiling. Reduce heat and simmer, uncovered, until mixture is medium

sauce consistency, about 15 minutes. Remove from heat; stir in basil. Pour sauce over spaghetti and toss; stir in Parmesan cheese.

3. Heat oven to 350° F. Spray 9-inch springform pan with cooking spray; coat with breadcrumbs. Line bottom and side of pan with ¾ of egg-plant slices, overlapping slices and allowing those on side to extend 1 to 1½ inches above top of pan. Spoon spaghetti mixture into pan; press into pan firmly. Fold eggplant slices at top of pan over spaghetti mixture. Overlap remaining eggplant slices on top, pressing firmly into place.

4. Bake, uncovered, until hot through, about 30 minutes. Remove sides of pan. Cut into wedges to serve.

Nutritional Data

PER SERVING		EXCHANGES	
Calories	372	Milk	0.0
% Calories from fat	13	Veg.	3.0
Fat (gm)	5.4	Fruit	0.0
Sat. Fat (gm)	1.4	Bread	3.5
Cholesterol (mg)	3.3	Meat	0.0
Sodium (mg)	139	Fat	1.0
Protein (gm)	13.5		
Carbohydrate (gm)	70		

6
RISOTTO

The two secrets to a fine risotto are using Italian arborio rice and constant stirring during the cooking process—both necessary to achieve the creamy texture risotto is known for. Once only available in Italian markets or by mail order, arborio rice can now be purchased in many supermarkets.

SHRIMP AND MUSHROOM RISOTTO

Arborio rice, a short-grain rice grown in the Arborio region of Italy, can be purchased in Italian groceries and in many supermarkets with ethnic food sections. This rice is especially suited for making risotto, as it cooks to a wonderful "creaminess." Other longer-grained rices can be used, but the texture of the risotto will be less "creamy."

4 Entree Servings (about 1¹/₄ cups each)

Olive oil cooking spray
1 small onion, chopped
3 cloves garlic, minced
2 cups sliced mushrooms
1 teaspoon dried rosemary leaves
1 teaspoon dried thyme leaves
1¹/₂ cups arborio rice
1¹/₂ quarts canned low-salt chicken broth
8 ounces peeled, deveined shrimp
¹/₄ teaspoon pepper
2 tablespoons grated Parmesan cheese

1. Spray large saucepan with cooking spray; heat over medium heat until hot. Saute onions and garlic until tender, about 5 minutes. Add mushrooms and herbs; cook until tender, 5 to 7 minutes. Stir in rice; cook over medium heat until rice begins to brown, 2 to 3 minutes, stirring frequently.

2. Heat chicken broth just to boiling in medium saucepan; reduce heat to medium-low to keep broth hot. Add broth to rice mixture, ¹/₂ cup at a time, stirring constantly until broth is absorbed before adding next ¹/₂ cup. Continue process until rice is *al dente* and mixture is creamy, 20 to 25 minutes.

3. Stir shrimp and pepper into mixture during last 15 minutes of cooking time. Serve in bowls; sprinkle with cheese.

Nutritional Data

PER SERVING		EXCHANGES	
Calories	378	Milk	0.0
% Calories from fat	8	Veg.	1.0
Fat (gm)	3.2	Fruit	0.0
Sat. Fat (gm)	0.9	Bread	4.0
Cholesterol (mg)	89.5	Meat	1.0
Sodium (mg)	258	Fat	0.0
Protein (gm)	20.1		
Carbohydrate (gm)	65.1		

PORCINI RISOTTO

◆

*Use dried shiitaki or Chinese black mushrooms
if the porcini are not available.*

6 Side-Dish Servings *(about ⅔ cup each)*

¼ to ½ ounce dried porcini mushrooms
　　　　Hot water
　　　　Olive oil cooking spray
　　1 small onion, chopped
　　3 cloves garlic, minced
　　1 small tomato, seeded, chopped
　　1 teaspoon dried sage leaves
　¼ teaspoon dried thyme leaves
1½ cups arborio rice
1½ quarts canned low-salt chicken broth
　¼ cup grated Parmesan cheese
　¼ teaspoon pepper
　　2 tablespoons pine nuts, *or* slivered
　　　　almonds, toasted
　　2 tablespoons finely chopped fresh sage, *or*
　　　　parsley

1. Place mushrooms in bowl; pour hot water over to cover. Let stand until mushrooms are soft, about 15 minutes; drain, reserving liquid. Slice mushrooms, discarding any tough parts.

2. Spray large saucepan with cooking spray; heat over medium heat until hot. Saute mushrooms, onions, and garlic until tender, about 5 minutes. Stir in tomato, sage, and thyme; cook 2 to 3 minutes more. Stir in rice. Cook over medium heat until rice begins to brown, 2 to 3 minutes, stirring frequently.

3. Heat chicken broth and reserved porcini liquid to boiling in medium saucepan; reduce heat to medium-low to keep broth hot. Add broth to rice mixture, 1/2 cup at a time, stirring constantly until broth is absorbed before adding another 1/2 cup. Continue process until rice is *al dente* and mixture is creamy, 20 to 25 minutes.

4. Stir Parmesan cheese and pepper into risotto. Serve in bowls; sprinkle with pine nuts and parsley.

Nutritional Data

PER SERVING		EXCHANGES	
Calories	251	Milk	0.0
% Calories from fat	15	Veg.	1.0
Fat (gm)	4.2	Fruit	0.0
Sat. Fat (gm)	0.9	Bread	2.5
Cholesterol (mg)	3.3	Meat	0.0
Sodium (mg)	146	Fat	0.5
Protein (gm)	8.7		
Carbohydrate (gm)	44.5		

RISI BISI

Opinions vary as to whether Risi Bisi is a risotto or a thick soup. If you agree with the latter definition, use an additional 1/2 to 1 cup of broth to make the mixture a thick-soup consistency.

8 Side-Dish Servings (about 1/2 cup each)

Olive oil cooking spray
1 small onion, chopped
3 cloves garlic, minced
1 1/2 cups arborio rice
2 teaspoons dried basil leaves
1 1/2 quarts canned low-salt chicken broth
8 ounces frozen, thawed tiny peas
1/4 cup grated Parmesan cheese
1/4 teaspoon pepper

1. Spray large saucepan with cooking spray; heat over medium heat until hot. Saute onions and garlic until tender, about 5 minutes. Stir in rice and basil. Cook over medium heat until rice begins to brown, 2 to 3 minutes, stirring frequently.

2. Heat chicken broth to boiling in medium saucepan; reduce heat to medium-low to keep broth hot. Add broth to rice mixture, 1/2 cup at a

time, stirring constantly until broth is absorbed before adding another $^1/_2$ cup. Continue process until rice is *al dente* and mixture is creamy, 20 to 25 minutes.

3. Stir peas into risotto during last 10 minutes of cooking time. Stir in Parmesan cheese and pepper.

Nutritional Data

PER SERVING		EXCHANGES	
Calories	192	Milk	0.0
% Calories from fat	9	Veg.	0.5
Fat (gm)	1.8	Fruit	0.0
Sat. Fat (gm)	0.7	Bread	2.5
Cholesterol (mg)	2.5	Meat	0.0
Sodium (mg)	132	Fat	0.0
Protein (gm)	7.1		
Carbohydrate (gm)	35.8		

ITALIAN SAUSAGE AND BROCCOLI RISOTTO

◆

This risotto is enhanced with the addition of homemade Italian sausage, using ground turkey abundantly seasoned with spices and herbs.

6 Entree Servings (about 1¹/₂ cups each)

- 12 ounces ground turkey
- 1 teaspoon fennel seeds, crushed
- 1 teaspoon dried sage leaves
- 1 teaspoon dried thyme leaves
- $^1/_2$ teaspoon dried oregano leaves
- $^1/_4$ teaspoon ground allspice
- $^1/_8$ teaspoon ground mace
- $^1/_2$ teaspoon salt (optional)
- 1 small onion, chopped
- 2 cloves garlic, minced
- 1$^1/_2$ cups arborio rice
- 1$^1/_2$ quarts canned low-salt chicken broth
- 2 cups broccoli florets, steamed
- $^1/_2$ cup raisins
- 2 tablespoons grated Parmesan cheese (optional)

1. Mix turkey, herbs, spices, and salt; refrigerate 1 to 2 hours. Cook turkey mixture in large saucepan until browned; remove from saucepan and drain. Discard fat from saucepan.

2. Add onions and garlic to saucepan; saute until tender, about 5 minutes. Stir in rice; cook over medium heat until rice begins to brown, 2 to 3 minutes, stirring frequently.

3. Heat chicken broth to boiling in medium saucepan; reduce heat to medium-low to keep broth hot. Add broth to rice mixture, ½ cup at a time, stirring constantly until broth is absorbed before adding another ½ cup. Continue process until rice is *al dente*, 20 to 25 minutes.

4. Add reserved turkey mixture, broccoli, and raisins to risotto during last 10 minutes of cooking time. Serve in bowls; sprinkle with Parmesan cheese (optional).

Nutritional Data

PER SERVING		EXCHANGES	
Calories	322	Milk	0.0
% Calories from fat	16	Veg.	1.0
Fat (gm)	5.6	Fruit	0.5
Sat. Fat (gm)	1.3	Bread	2.5
Cholesterol (mg)	21.1	Meat	1.0
Sodium (mg)	101	Fat	0.5
Protein (gm)	14.6		
Carbohydrate (gm)	53.4		

SUMMER SQUASH RISOTTO

*A perfect risotto for summer, when squash and
tomatoes are garden-fresh.*

6 Side-Dish Servings

1 small zucchini, sliced
1 small yellow squash, sliced
2 teaspoons olive oil
1 small onion, chopped
2 cloves garlic, minced
4 Italian plum tomatoes, cut into fourths
1 teaspoon dried oregano leaves
³/₄ cup arborio rice
3 cups canned low-salt chicken broth
2 tablespoons grated Romano cheese
¹/₄ teaspoon pepper

1. Saute zucchini and yellow squash in oil in large saucepan until crisp-tender, 5 to 7 minutes; remove from saucepan and reserve.

2. Add onions and garlic to saucepan; saute until tender, about 5 minutes. Add tomatoes and oregano; cook until tomatoes are soft, about 3 minutes. Add rice; cook over medium heat until rice begins to brown, 2 to 3 minutes.

3. Heat chicken broth to boiling in small saucepan; reduce heat to medium-low to keep broth hot. Add broth to rice mixture, ¹/₂ cup at a time, stirring constantly, until broth is absorbed before adding another ¹/₂ cup. Continue process until rice is *al dente*, 20 to 25 minutes.

4. Add reserved squash to risotto during last few minutes of cooking time. Stir in Romano cheese and pepper.

Nutritional Data

PER SERVING		EXCHANGES	
Calories	152	Milk	0.0
% Calories from fat	18	Veg.	1.0
Fat (gm)	3.1	Fruit	0.0
Sat. Fat (gm)	0.7	Bread	1.5
Cholesterol (mg)	2.4	Meat	0.0
Sodium (mg)	70	Fat	0.5
Protein (gm)	4.8		
Carbohydrate (gm)	27		

7
ASIAN NOODLES

Asian noodles, now more readily available in supermarkets, allow our pasta repertory to include some interesting oriental dishes. In China, noodles are symbolic of longevity and are often served as the main dish at birthday meals. As the symbol of longevity, the noodles are very long—they are never made short. If oriental noodles are not available, American or Italian thin spaghetti or linguine may be substituted.

ORIENTAL SOUP WITH NOODLES AND CHICKEN

*The dried chow mein noodles are not the fried
ones we have used with chop suey for many years.
Be sure the correct noodles are used.*

4 Side-Dish Servings (about ³/₄ cup each)

1 ounce oriental dried cloud ears, *or* ¹/₂ ounce
  dried shiitaki mushrooms
  Hot water
  Olive oil cooking spray
¹/₂ cup julienne carrots
2 cans (14¹/₂ ounces each) low-salt
  chicken broth
2 tablespoons dry sherry (optional)
1¹/₂ teaspoons light soy sauce
¹/₄ teaspoon five-spice powder
8 ounces boneless, skinless chicken breast,
  cooked, shredded
2 ounces snow peas
¹/₂ cup sliced mushrooms
¹/₂ package (5 ounce-size) dried chow mein
  noodles
¹/₄ teaspoon salt (optional)
¹/₄ teaspoon pepper

1. Place dried mushrooms in bowl; pour hot water over to cover. Let
stand until mushrooms are soft, about 15 minutes; drain. Slice mushrooms, discarding any tough parts.

2. Spray large saucepan with cooking spray; heat over medium heat until
hot. Saute dried mushrooms and carrots 3 to 4 minutes. Add chicken
broth, sherry, soy sauce, and five-spice powder. Heat to boiling; reduce
heat and simmer, covered, 10 minutes. Stir in chicken, snow peas, and
sliced mushrooms; cook until peas are crisp-tender, about 4 minutes.

3. Add noodles to saucepan; cook until noodles are just tender, about 10
minutes. Stir in salt and pepper.

Nutritional Data

PER SERVING		EXCHANGES	
Calories	213	Milk	0.0
% Calories from fat	30	Veg.	0.5
Fat (gm)	7.6	Fruit	0.0
Sat. Fat (gm)	1.2	Bread	1.0
Cholesterol (mg)	29.2	Meat	1.5
Sodium (mg)	259	Fat	1.0
Protein (gm)	16.4		
Carbohydrate (gm)	19.7		

SESAME NOODLE SOUP WITH VEGETABLES

Use oriental sesame oil, which is dark in color and concentrated in flavor; light-colored sesame oil is very delicate in flavor. The fresh Chinese-style noodles are sometimes called soup noodles, chow mein noodles, or spaghetti. Caution: fresh noodles cook very quickly.

4 Entree Servings (about 2 cups each)

1/2 cup sliced green onions and tops
4 cloves garlic, minced
1 tablespoon sesame oil
2 cups Napa cabbage, chopped or thinly sliced
1 cup chopped red bell pepper
1/2 cup julienne carrots
3 cans (14 1/2 ounces each) low-salt chicken broth
12 ounces boneless, skinless chicken breast, cooked, shredded
1 package (12 ounces) fresh Chinese-style noodles
1/2 teaspoon salt (optional)
1/4 teaspoon pepper

1. Saute green onions and garlic in sesame oil in large saucepan until tender, about 5 minutes. Add cabbage, bell pepper, and carrots; saute until vegetables are crisp-tender, about 5 minutes.

2. Add chicken broth to saucepan; heat to boiling. Stir in chicken and noodles; return to boiling. Reduce heat and simmer, uncovered, until noodles are just tender, 1 to 2 minutes. Stir in salt (optional) and pepper.

Nutritional Data

PER SERVING		EXCHANGES	
Calories	302	Milk	0.0
% Calories from fat	19	Veg.	1.5
Fat (gm)	6.5	Fruit	0.0
Sat. Fat (gm)	1	Bread	2.0
Cholesterol (mg)	43.5	Meat	2.0
Sodium (mg)	144	Fat	0.0
Protein (gm)	23		
Carbohydrate (gm)	37.8		

VIETNAMESE CURRIED CHICKEN AND COCONUT SOUP

Rice noodles, made with rice flour, can be round or flat. They must be softened in water before cooking. Angel hair pasta can be substituted.

6 Servings (about 1¹/₄ cups each)

	Vegetable cooking spray
1	tablespoon minced garlic
3 to 4	tablespoons curry powder
2	cans (14¹/₂ ounces each) low-fat chicken broth
3	cups reduced-fat coconut milk
2	tablespoons minced ginger root
²/₃	cup sliced green onions and tops
1	tablespoon minced parsley
1	tablespoon grated lime rind
¹/₂ to 1	teaspoon oriental chili paste
1	pound boneless, skinless chicken breast
¹/₄	cup lime juice
¹/₃	cup minced cilantro
	Salt and white pepper, to taste
¹/₂	package (8-ounce size) rice noodles

1. Spray large saucepan with cooking spray; heat over medium heat until hot. Saute garlic 1 minute; stir in curry powder and cook, stirring constantly, 30 seconds. Add chicken broth, coconut milk, ginger root, onions, parsley, lime rind, and chili paste; heat to boiling.

2. Add chicken breasts and return to boiling. Reduce heat and simmer, covered, until chicken is cooked, about 20 minutes. Remove chicken. Shred chicken breast with 2 forks. Return to saucepan. Stir in lime juice and cilantro; season to taste with salt and white pepper. Simmer about 5 minutes longer.

3. Place noodles in large bowl; pour cold water over to cover. Let stand until noodles are separate and soft, about 5 minutes; drain. Stir noodles into 4 quarts boiling water. Reduce heat and simmer, uncovered, until tender, about 5 minutes; drain.

4. Spoon noodles into soup bowls; ladle soup over noodles.

Nutritional Data

PER SERVING		EXCHANGES	
Calories	261	Milk	0.0
% Calories from fat	29	Veg.	1.0
Fat (gm)	8.5	Fruit	0.0
Sat. fat (gm)	0.6	Bread	1.0
Cholesterol (mg)	46	Meat	2.5
Sodium (mg)	347	Fat	0.5
Protein (gm)	23		
Carbohydrate (gm)	23.4		

STIR-FRIED RICE NOODLES WITH SHRIMP

*Rice noodles are also called cellophane noodles,
or bihon. The dried noodles are soaked in cold water
to soften, then drained before using.*

4 Entree Servings (about 1½ cups each)

1 package (8 ounces) rice noodles
Cold water
1 tablespoon vegetable oil
8 ounces peeled, deveined shrimp
4 green onions, thinly sliced
1 tablespoon finely chopped fresh ginger root
2 cups shredded Napa cabbage
1 cup canned low-salt chicken broth
2 tablespoons dry sherry (optional)
2 to 3 teaspoons light soy sauce
½ to 1 teaspoon Szechwan chili sauce

1. Place noodles in large bowl; pour cold water over to cover. Let stand until noodles separate and are soft, about 5 minutes; drain.

2. Heat oil in wok or skillet over medium-high heat until hot. Add shrimp, green onions, and ginger root. Stir-fry until shrimp are pink and cooked; remove from wok.

3. Add cabbage to wok; stir-fry just until cabbage turns bright in color, about 1 minute. Stir in drained noodles and shrimp; add chicken broth, sherry, soy sauce, and chili sauce. Heat to boiling; reduce heat and simmer, uncovered, until noodles have absorbed all liquid, about 5 minutes.

Nutritional Data

PER SERVING		EXCHANGES	
Calories	292	Milk	0.0
% Calories from fat	13	Veg.	1.0
Fat (gm)	4.2	Fruit	0.0
Sat. Fat (gm)	0.6	Bread	3.0
Cholesterol (mg)	87.1	Meat	1.0
Sodium (mg)	223	Fat	0.0
Protein (gm)	17.1		
Carbohydrate (gm)	46.6		

ORIENTAL NOODLE SALAD

◆

*If you enjoy the flavor of sesame oil, substitute
2 teaspoons sesame oil and 1 tablespoon plus 1
teaspoon vegetable oil for the olive oil.*

8 Side-Dish Servings (about 1/2 cup each)

- 2/3 package (12 ounce-size) rice noodles
  Cold water
- 4 quarts boiling water
- 2 cups snow peas, steamed
- 2 cups sliced red bell pepper
- 2 medium oranges, peeled, cut into segments
- 1 cup sliced mushrooms
- 1/2 cup fresh or canned bean sprouts, rinsed and drained
- 1/3 cup orange juice
- 2 tablespoons olive oil
- 2 cloves garlic, minced
- 1/2 teaspoon five-spice powder
- 1/4 teaspoon salt
- 1/4 teaspoon pepper

1. Place noodles in large bowl; pour cold water over to cover. Let stand until noodles separate and are soft, about 5 minutes. Stir noodles into 4 quarts boiling water. Reduce heat and simmer, uncovered, until tender, about 5 minutes; drain and cool.

2. Combine noodles, snow peas, bell pepper, oranges, mushrooms, and bean sprouts in large bowl. Combine in small bowl, orange juice and remaining ingredients; pour over noodle mixture and toss.

Nutritional Data

PER SERVING		EXCHANGES	
Calories	198	Milk	0.0
% Calories from fat	16	Veg.	0.5
Fat (gm)	3.7	Fruit	0.5
Sat. Fat (gm)	0.5	Bread	2.0
Cholesterol (mg)	0	Meat	0.0
Sodium (mg)	72	Fat	0.5
Protein (gm)	5.9		
Carbohydrate (gm)	36.9		

ASIAN-STYLE NOODLE SALAD

♦

Enjoy the wonderful blending of flavors in this salad. Thin spaghetti or linguine can be substituted for the fresh Asian egg noodles.

4 Servings

- 8 ounces fresh Chinese-style noodles, *or* thin spaghetti, *or* linguine, cooked
- 1 cup fat-free plain yogurt
- 1/4 cup reduced-fat peanut butter
- 2 tablespoons rice wine vinegar
- 1 tablespoon reduced-sodium tamari soy sauce
- 1 teaspoon toasted sesame oil
- 1 tablespoon sugar
- 1 tablespoon minced ginger root
- 1/2 teaspoon 5-spice powder
- 1/2 teaspoon minced garlic
- 1/2 teaspoon cayenne pepper
- 1 cup shredded carrots
- 1 medium cucumber, peeled, seeded, cubed
- 1/2 cup chopped red bell pepper
- 1/4 cup sliced green onions and tops
- 1/4 cup finely chopped cilantro
  Lettuce leaves, as garnish

1. Cook noodles in 4 quarts boiling water until just tender, 1 to 2 minutes (if using spaghetti or linguine, cook according to package directions). Drain and cool to room temperature.

2. Mix yogurt, peanut butter, vinegar, soy sauce, sesame oil, sugar, ginger root, and seasonings in bowl until smooth. Spoon dressing over noodles and toss. Add remaining ingredients, except lettuce, and toss. Spoon salad into lettuce-lined serving bowl.

Nutritional Data

PER SERVING		EXCHANGES	
Calories	388	Milk	0.0
% Calories from fat	17	Veg.	3.0
Fat (gm)	7.7	Fruit	0.0
Sat. fat (gm)	1.5	Bread	3.5
Cholesterol (mg)	1	Meat	0.0
Sodium (mg)	242	Fat	1.5
Protein (gm)	14.3		
Carbohydrate (gm)	67.3		

RICE NOODLES AND PORK WITH GREENS

Tender rice noodles and pork tenderloin are bedded on greens.

4 Servings

- 1/2 package (4-ounce size) rice noodles
  Vegetable cooking spray
- 12 ounces pork tenderloin, cut into
  1/8-inch-thick slices
- 4 cups mesclun, *or* other mixed greens
- 1/4 cup finely chopped mint leaves
- 1/4 cup finely chopped cilantro leaves
- 1 cup peeled, seeded, diced cucumber
  Lime Dressing (recipe follows)

1. Place noodles in large bowl; pour cold water over to cover. Let stand until noodles are separate and soft, about 5 minutes; drain. Stir noodles into 4 quarts boiling water. Reduce heat and simmer, uncovered, until tender, about 5 minutes; drain. Cool.

2. Spray medium skillet with cooking spray; heat over medium heat until hot. Add pork and cook until browned, 2 to 3 minutes on each side.

3. Combine mesclun, herbs, and cucumber and arrange on 4 large salad plates. Top each serving with rice noodles and pork. Spoon warm Lime Dressing over.

Lime Dressing

Makes about 3/4 cup

- 1/2 cup water
- 1/2 cup lime juice
- 1 teaspoon cornstarch
- 2 tablespoons sugar
- 2 teaspoons minced garlic
- 2 to 3 teaspoons reduced-sodium tamari soy sauce
- 1 teaspoon dark sesame oil
- 1 teaspoon black bean sauce
- 1/2 teaspoon hot chili paste

1. Combine water, lime juice, and cornstarch in small saucepan; stir in remaining ingredients. Heat to boiling; boil, whisking constantly, until thickened, about 1 minute.

Nutritional Data

PER SERVING		EXCHANGES	
Calories	220	Milk	0.0
% Calories from fat	19	Veg.	2.0
Fat (gm)	4.4	Fruit	0.0
Sat. fat (gm)	1.2	Bread	1.0
Cholesterol (mg)	49.1	Meat	2.0
Sodium (mg)	244	Fat	0.0
Protein (gm)	20.9		
Carbohydrate (gm)	24.2		

BEEF AND VEGETABLE LO MEIN

To store leftover ginger root, place it in a jar, fill with dry sherry, cover, and refrigerate; the ginger root will last at least 6 months. Ginger root does not have to be peeled before using.

4 Entree Servings

 1 package (12 ounces) fresh Chinese-style noodles
 4 quarts boiling water
 4 Chinese dried black *or* shiitaki mushrooms
   Hot water
 1 tablespoon sesame oil, *or* vegetable oil
 1 tablespoon finely chopped fresh ginger root
 3 cloves garlic, minced
12 ounces eye of round steak, excess fat trimmed, cut into 1/2-inch strips
 2 cups broccoli florets
 1 cup sliced carrots
1/3 cup water
 2 tablespoons dry sherry, *or* water
 2 teaspoons cornstarch
 1 tablespoon black bean paste
 2 teaspoons light soy sauce

1. Cook noodles in 4 quarts boiling water until tender, about 2 minutes; drain and reserve. Place dried mushrooms in bowl; pour hot water over to cover. Let stand until mushrooms are soft, about 15 minutes; drain. Slice mushrooms, discarding tough parts.

2. Heat oil in wok or skillet over medium-high heat until hot. Stir-fry mushrooms, ginger, and garlic 2 minutes. Add beef; stir-fry until beef is cooked, about 5 minutes. Remove from wok.

3. Add broccoli and carrots to wok; stir-fry until vegetables are crisp-tender, 5 to 8 minutes. Remove from wok.

4. Combine ⅓ cup water, sherry, and cornstarch; add to wok and heat to boiling. Boil, stirring constantly, until thickened, about 1 minute. Stir in black bean paste and soy sauce. Return beef and vegetable mixtures to wok; add noodles. Stir-fry over medium heat until hot through, 2 to 3 minutes.

Nutritional Data

PER SERVING		EXCHANGES	
Calories	300	Milk	0.0
% Calories from fat	18	Veg.	1.0
Fat (gm)	6	Fruit	0.0
Sat. Fat (gm)	1.4	Bread	2.0
Cholesterol (mg)	41.2	Meat	2.5
Sodium (mg)	153	Fat	0.0
Protein (gm)	22.1		
Carbohydrate (gm)	37.9		

INDEX